REGENERATING GENERATIONS

Denise,
Colleague in ministry
Life-long learner
Alan

AF807620

An Adventure in Vital Living

Evelyn Johnson & Alan Forsman
with Reji Laberje

HOW DO CHURCHES ADDRESS THE AGE WAVE OF TSUNAMI PROPORTIONS?

Are you ready to regenerate?

As a Baby Boomer who has just entered the world of retirement, I am already experiencing some of the losses related to aging. My challenge is to embrace the process of aging and to discover how I can continue to use the gifts and abilities God has given me. I want to be part of a church community that will encourage me to keep growing. ***"Regenerating Generations"*** *will equip church leaders (and individuals) to plan for those later years—and to create effective ministries for, by, and with older adults.*

~Millie Lungren
Served as Director of the Covenant Resource Center,
Associate Director of Adult Ministries
Evangelical Covenant Church

I would trust Evelyn and Alan to work with any church on any topic. I particularly trust Alan and Evelyn to help release the untapped and latent potential trapped in the Baby Boomer and older generations.

~Dr. John Jackson
President of William Jessup University
Author of "High Impact Church Planting"
and other Pastoral Resources

*"**Regenerating Generations**" is a compelling and thoughtful guide to planning ministries for older adults and to guide Baby Boomers through their next phase of life. This is a go-to book for church leaders who want to effectively minister to the sixty-five and older age group.*

~Terri Cunliffe
President, Covenant Retirement Communities

*Two people most influential in beginning our older adult ministry at Peninsula Covenant Church were Evelyn Johnson, our denominational leader, and Alan Forsman, our church consultant. Evelyn brought a vision for our church and Alan helped us to put it in place. Thanks to them it worked and PLUS ministries became a reality. "**Regenerating Generations**" can bring the same successful "adventure" to other churches.*

~Rod Toews
Resident, Covenant Village of Turlock

*I am excited that Alan Forsman and Evelyn Johnson are providing this resource, "**Regenerating Generations**", for churches to explore the opportunities and challenges for ministry to older adults! Alan is a skillful communicator and he is passionate about helping churches and individuals to engage in visioning and planning. I know that his expertise and experience, together with that of Evelyn Johnson, will provide inspiration and practical ideas for Christians seeking* *to minister to the exploding population of older adults in our communities.*

~Elsa Cisar
Divisional Social Services Director,
The Salvation Army - Del Oro Division

As the world around us experiences rapid change, the wisdom, savvy, and spiritual maturity of older members of the Christian community is desperately needed by its younger members. I know of no better guides to help animate and unleash this potential than Evelyn Johnson and Alan Forsman.

~Dr. David P. Nystrom
Professor in Residence, Western Seminary Campus
Author of five books including: "James in the NIV," Application Commentary Series, and "History of Christianity"

With aging demographics and increased longevity, preparing church leaders and Baby Boomers, themselves, for a Third Stage in life becomes a very pressing need for churches, their leaders, and for individuals. Evelyn and Alan are well prepared to provide guidance to this generation of which they are members. I look forward to implementing the advice of ***"Regenerating Generations"*** *in my own post retirement life.*

~Dr. Dean Lundgren
Served as Chief Financial Officer, Evangelical Covenant Church

Evelyn Johnson and Alan Forsman are gifted leaders, teachers, and facilitators in both the church and nonprofit sectors. They both bring a unique blend of practitioner based wisdom and highly-skilled process and plan implementation. ***"Regenerating Generations"*** *is a timely book that will help the church leverage the significant demographic and generational shift towards greater Missional endeavor.*

~Dr. David W. Kersten
Dean, North Park Theological Seminary

Evelyn Johnson and Alan Forsman have been a formidable team for decades. When you combine their brilliance with their practicality, you can be sure that the result will be transformational. When their attention is focused on the church, especially the most significant growing edge of the church, you have a book like ***"Regenerating Generations".*** *It is nothing short of a must read for those organizations that want to stay on the cutting edge of significant and eternal ministry that will make an impact for generations.*

~Kreig Gammelgard
Associate Superintendant, Director of Congregational Vitality
East Coast Conference

ISBN-10: 0692758453
ISBN-13: 978-0692758458

Library of Congress Control Number: 2016913334
Reji Laberje Writing and Publishing, Waukesha, WI

BISAC Codes:
REL109010 Religion/Christian Ministry/Adult
REL095000 Religion/Christian Education/Adult
REL074000 Religion/Christian Ministry/Pastoral Resources

Writing and Publishing
www.rejilaberje.com

Copyright © 2016 by Evelyn Johnson and Alan Forsman

All rights reserved. No part of this book may be reproduced or transmitted in any form or by any means, electronic or mechanical, including: photocopying, recording, or by any information storage and retrieval system, without permission in writing from the copyright owners.

This work is based on the experiences of individuals. Every effort has been made to ensure the accuracy of the content.

Quantity order requests can be emailed to:

publishing@rejilaberje.com

Or mailed to:

Reji Laberje Writing and Publishing

Publishing Orders

234 W. Broadway Street

Waukesha, WI 53186

Johnson, Evelyn and Forsman, Alan

Regenerating Generations – An Adventure in Vital Living

Contributing Author: Reji Laberje, Reji Laberje Writing and Publishing

Contributing Editor: Marla McKenna

Interior Design: Reji Laberje

Cover Design: Michael Nicloy

Photos: Kimberly Laberge

DEDICATION

This book is dedicated to all those who have rejected the ageist stereotypes and modeled for me vital living all the days of their lives. And, it is also dedicated to my grandchildren who help me stay in touch with the "reality" of a changing world.

~Evelyn

This book is dedicated to all those who modeled for me, and taught me, vital aging through their significant lives.

~Alan

Foreword

The seeds for this book were planted when I was a child as I was observing models of persons who were living vital lives, many of whom were sixty and over. This blessing of older persons modeling vital living has continued throughout my life.

In my late twenties, I met Hildegard, a woman who was forty years older than me. She became, not only a close friend, but a spiritual mentor for twenty-nine years until her death in 1997. Hildegard modeled for me what it meant to live into God's calling all the days of one's life.

In my late thirties, I began engaging with our denomination's ministries with older adults and those preparing for retirement. The committee work and related writing broadened my understanding of the potential within the last stage of life. Experiencing the reality of aging parents and, later, being a caregiver for my husband in his later years were means by which God taught me about aging, particularly acceptance of physical losses.

My sister, brother, sisters-in-law, and brother-in-law model for me what it means to live vital lives well into the eighties. My sister, now in her late eighties, works full-time overseeing a hardware business.

In summer 2015, after stepping aside from compensated employment, I found a new freedom to pursue passions that had been somewhat dormant. One of those passions was connecting the church in more meaningful ways with the existing sixty-five and over population, as well as the Boomers preparing for this next phase of life. Thus, I rejoiced in this opportunity to engage in visioning and planning with my ministry colleague, Alan Forsman, with whom I have pursued many new initiatives for more than thirty years. ***"Regenerating Generations"*** *is a God-given opportunity for us to assist church leaders in a new way.*

~Evelyn Johnson

~~~~

The positive influence of grandparents shaped my understanding of vital aging and those early lessons stayed with me throughout my life.

As a youngster, I was not articulate about the aging process, but I listened and observed grandparents at their different stages of aging and was impressed by their activity and vigor. In reflecting, I never really thought of them as "old."

I was fortunate to have two sets of grandparents in my early developmental years. I sat with them, played games with them, talked with them, worked with them, traveled with them, and was as engaged in their lives, as they were in mine.

My grandparents and I were connected, in many ways, well into my adult years. Death eventually claimed all of them, as it does, but they left a significant legacy.

During early graduate school I completed some course work in gerontology and I found it fascinating.

While serving churches I started four older adult ministries.

My Doctoral dissertation was shaped by my work with older adults.
~~~~

Over the years I have had the opportunity to teach university classes on the subject of vital aging, as well as consult with churches and organizations that work directly with our increasingly aging population. All of these experiences have been enriching and I have received much more than I have given. I am pleased and honored that I am able to continue learning and serving in this significant field and elsewhere.

"Regenerating Generations" *is as much a call as any work I've accomplished in the field, alongside my longtime colleague, Evelyn Johnson.*

~Alan Forsman

Table of Contents

About This Book

"Regenerating Generations" *is a Reji Laberje Writing and Publishing interactive text. In this book, you will find QR codes that will provide insight into what is being shared. Find a free QR scanner for your smart device via a search through your device's app store. Scan the inserted QR codes with your smart device to discover online resources. Further information from the QR codes can be found on the Electronic Resource Hub (ERH) for* **Eval Ministries** *at:*

http://www.rejilaberje.com/eval-ministries.html

INTRODUCTION

We are facing an age wave of tsunami proportions. Approximately 10,000 Baby Boomers have been turning sixty-five each day since 2011, and this trend will continue through 2029. The sixty-five and over population will increase from about fourteen percent of the total population in 2015 to twenty percent in 2030 per the U.S. Census Bureau projections in 2012[1].

It is time for church leaders to envision, plan, and implement *significant* experiences for older adults and those preparing for retirement and beyond.

> IT IS TIME FOR CHURCH LEADERS TO ENVISION, PLAN, AND IMPLEMENT SIGNIFICANT EXPERIENCES FOR OLDER ADULTS AND THOSE PREPARING FOR RETIREMENT AND BEYOND.

The retirement age of sixty-five has been a standard across the nation for many years, but things are changing; one size does not fit all. Many people continue to work beyond the traditional retirement age, often due to limited savings. For

---

[1] *Ortman, Jennifer M., Victoria A. Velkoff, and Howard Hogan. "An Aging Nation: The Older Population in the United States." U.S. Census Bureau, May 2014. Web. June 2016.*

those born in 1959 and after, full benefits from Social Security are not available now until age sixty-seven. Some choose phased retirement while others move onto second careers. Many continue working for the meaning and satisfaction derived from the experience. Many organizations are facing a loss of tribal knowledge within their companies as a result of the exit of aging Baby Boomers, so skilled people are being asked to stay on the job.

A prevailing attitude suggests that being older is mostly about decline. Our society has constructed a system that furthers ageism just as it created and maintained systems that perpetuate racism and sexism.

AGEISM

[EY-JIZ-*UH*M]

NOUN

a tendency to regard older persons as debilitated, unworthy of attention, or unsuitable for employment

(From Dictionary.com)

Although there *are* losses, opportunities to create one's future are possible. In reality, aging begins when we are born. We are aging as much at age seven as we are at age seventy. If we stop aging, we are no longer living. The key question is *How well are we embracing the process of aging at whatever age or stage?*

Another factor that plays into personally embracing aging is the concept of psychological age. We tend to see ourselves younger than we really are. Sometimes, this may be as much as a fifteen-year difference. (Sixty-five is the new fifty!)

Adding to all of these realities is the desire among many to "age in place," or stay in their current living situations, even as needs change. Nearly ninety percent of the sixty-five and older population want to age in place[1].

Aging in place long-term will potentially require in-home assistance. Families and community senior services cannot come close to meeting the needs of the current age wave. In 2013, approximately 34.2 million Americans provided unpaid care to an adult aged fifty or older who needed help with daily activities according to the American Association of Retired Persons (AARP) Public Policy Institute. That number will only increase!

Vital living is a desired outcome for older adults wherever they choose to live, whether in their home, with family or friends, or in a retirement community. Vital living includes a sense of well-being, both physically and emotionally, the freedom to be oneself, and a commitment to carry out one's life purpose. Vital living requires engagement. A community is needed.

VITAL LIVING INCLUDES A SENSE OF WELL-BEING, BOTH PHYSICALLY AND EMOTIONALLY, THE FREEDOM TO BE ONESELF, AND A COMMITMENT TO CARRY OUT ONE'S LIFE PURPOSE.

---

1 AARP Public Policy Institute and National Conference of State Legislatures Research Report, 2011

The local church is the ideal entity to partner with the aging population, both before and after persons step aside from compensated employment and/or the demands of managing a household. There is a need for effective ministries not just *for* older adults, but also *with* them and *by* them. It is not merely important to serve older adults, but also to allow them to continue serving. Early planning for later years must be a priority.

Author Paul Tournier, in "*Learn to Grow Old*", postulated that we should challenge people in their forties and fifties to begin thinking and planning for the next thirty to forty years. Given the increase in life expectancy, that estimate today would be "forty to fifty years." To date, sadly, most churches have not been leaders in meeting this need. Society is setting the pace with the birth of numerous new organizations such as Encore, in addition to a revamped AARP. As children of God and stewards of life, we have a responsibility to join in this movement and become leaders bringing the message of hope that extends beyond this life on earth.

This book is written for local church leaders and those of us who are to assume responsibility in addressing the possibilities for meeting the needs of older adults. We acknowledge that the references to statistics and trends reflect data from within the United States. Although Alaska and Hawaii are included within that data, the reality of diversity in these contexts must be considered in application. The Canadian context is not described within the book, but there are indications of similar trends in Canada, even exceeding percentages quoted for the United States in some areas. Church leaders in Canada are encouraged to access the updates from the Canadian Longitudinal Study on Aging (CLSA)[1]. This study was launched several years ago, as a national, long-term study with an aim to find ways to help Canadians live long and live well, and to understand why some age in healthy fashion, while others do not.

"Regenerating Generations" is divided into several parts:

- Part I—an overview of Biblical references to old age, historical reflections on retirement, trends in population projections for older adults, myths related to growing old, critical dimensions of psychological and spiritual preparation for the last phase of adulthood, and stories of persons who are models of vital living
- Part II—a framework for wholistic ministry by, with, and for older adults, a planning process, and starter ministry ideas
- Part III—a compilation of good news stories from pioneers; the input is from leaders with whom we have had direct contact as they engaged in various stages of their process
- Part IV—some final thoughts, resources, and research sites

There is much on the horizon to celebrate, anticipate, and create. ***Let's wake up, join these pioneers, and go confidently into the future!***

---

[1] *"Canadian Longitudinal Study on Aging." Web. June 2016.*

PART I

PREPARE ONESELF

Uncharted leadership is absolutely dependent on the leader's own ongoing exploration, learning, and transformation.

~"Canoeing the Mountains" Tod Bolsinger

CHAPTER 1

Setting the Stage

What got you here, won't get you there.
~Marshall Goldsmith

Is it evolution or revolution?

Which concept best describes the development of retirement and the unfortunate side effect of a marginalized segment of our population today?

Dictionary.com defines retirement: the act of retiring, withdrawing, or leaving; the state of being retired. When one reads the word, "withdrawing," it's hard not to conjure a negative image; it's akin to retreating, or backing down. Who really wants to back down from life? Perhaps this is why retirement was never mentioned in the Bible.

On the contrary, in Biblical times, those referenced as old, advanced in years, full of days, or elderly, continued to live their callings, engaging in whatever ways God directed them in much the same manners as their younger counterparts. Our modern concept of retirement is completely unknown in the Bible.

Throughout God's Word, the aged are cited as resourceful people with valuable gifts to share for the good of everyone.

In Exodus 7:7 (NIV), Moses and Aaron as chosen to lead the Israelites out of Egyptian bondage at the ages of **eighty** and **eighty-three**.

Caleb, who accompanied Joshua to the Promised Land, exclaimed, *"So here I am today,* ***eighty-five years old!*** *I am still as strong today as the day Moses sent me out; I'm just as vigorous to go out to battle now as I was then."* (Joshua 14:10-11 NIV)

Daniel was over **eighty** when he served as one of the governors of Babylon and was thrown into the lion's den[1].

Zacharias and Elizabeth were both "**advanced in years**" when John the Baptist was born. (Luke 1:7 NIV)

Simeon and Anna bore witness to the Christ child in their **eighties**! (Luke 2:28-38 NIV)

These are only a few of the many references to the benefits and blessings of lifetime service.

If we're honest with ourselves, I doubt many would look to our octogenarians to be leaders in the wilderness, scouts to an unknown land, heads of state, new parents, or even—sadly—reliable witnesses. The Bible didn't discount a person due to the natural process of aging. Although there is reference to infirmities occurring with old age, such as blindness and decreased mobility, none of these issues were noted as interferences with an individual's pursuit of and engagement with God's direction for their lives. When a person was blessed to continue living, the individual assumed it was to be purposeful.

> THE BIBLE DIDN'T DISCOUNT A PERSON DUE TO THE NATURAL PROCESS OF AGING.

[1] *Daniel: An Expositional Commentary*, James Montgomery Boice, 2003.

~~~~

Secular history has a different story to tell. Longevity of years declined in the early centuries, but—by medieval times—the numbers of the elderly population had increased to a point of reaching critical mass. Older people were everywhere giving advice, trying to help, and often, the real problem, holding onto wealth.

Chancellor Otto Van Bismarck of Germany is credited with the actual introduction of retirement in the 1800s. In 1881, Van Bismarck introduced the concept as a way to help those who could not work productively due to age or incapacity; he noted that they have a right to be provided with care. In 1889 the government approved paying a pension to any nonworking German over the age of seventy, an action that had a very limited consequence financially because few lived beyond seventy-years at that time. Nonetheless, it was an action that brought attention to when old age *begins*. It also established the precedent of a government paying people for growing old – a form of "old age" insurance.

During the same time period, private pension plans began to emerge in the United States with over three hundred reported by 1920. The growth in the number of pension plans was attributed to employers' desire to attract and retain workers, as well as providing a more humane way to remove an older, less productive employee. The German concept of retirement proved most helpful to employers in the United States in the 1890s and early 1900s as the
~~~~

country experienced a shift from an agrarian society to an increasingly industrial society.

When agriculture dominated the economy, there was no stopping an individual until he or she was physically incapable of doing the work. A farmer kept working, often assigning the physically demanding tasks to younger family members or hired hands.

The year 1920 was an historical tipping point in the United States. It was the first time in the country's history that more people were living in cities than in the country. As city factories replaced farms in economic importance, the question emerged as to whether older employees were slowing down production or occupying positions that resulted in increasing unemployment among younger workers.

It seemed that the only way to get the older persons to stop working for pay was to pay them enough to quit working. Thus, the Social Security Act of 1935 was enacted establishing age sixty-five as the "normal" retirement age. This new retirement age and provision of an "old age" insurance was viewed as a matter of caring for the elderly. At the time of the enactment of the 1935 Social Security Act, the actuarial studies showed that sixty-five was an appropriate age and the overall financial implications were manageable. At the time, for those just *born*, sixty was the life expectancy. For those who lived to age sixty-five, they could expect to live another twelve years. Thus, "retirees" were few and they would receive these new Social Security benefits for a minimal time. Plus, of course, they would have contributed to that which they would receive.

The financial expectations of those who initiated and approved the Social Security Act did not prove to be on target. With medical advances and greater attention to wellness, the lifespan of older adults expanded quickly and significantly. Increasingly (though perhaps unrelatable by today's standard), retired people wished they could work. The opposite of work was play, but funding leisure activities seemed to be reserved for those with accumulated wealth.

In the late 1960s the Age Discrimination in Employment Act (ADEA) was enacted to prohibit age discrimination in employment for individuals, but it did not initially apply to individuals over age sixty-five nor did it prohibit mandatory retirement. The evolution of ADEA over the next fifty years became indicative of western societies' extended life expectancies. In 1987, the upper age limit was removed and mandatory provisions were banned, with a few exceptions, such as military members and similar public service functions.

During the same time period that the government was addressing age discrimination (in 1983), the normal retirement age of the Social Security Act was raised from what became the "traditional" sixty-five. There were years of incremental month increases in age until the current provision for full benefits at age sixty-seven for all individuals born after 1959.

Was it too late? After a century, the cultural expectation for leaving the work force was already formed.

Evolution or revolution?

We can say the concept of retirement *evolved* slowly and naturally, yet the reality of revolution is also very much a part of the big picture.

Both the German actions in the late 1880s and the U.S. action in 1935 were rooted in concerns for economic security and care for the elderly combined with a pending crisis of many unemployed young workers. The Social Security Act of 1935[1], in particular, can be cited as **an action to remove older workers with no justifiable reason** other than chronological age.

How have we strayed so far from a biblical beginning, when every person, regardless of age, continued to engage in purposeful living, to an expectation that—at a certain age—we will withdraw and leave?

> HOW HAVE WE STRAYED SO FAR FROM A BIBLICAL BEGINNING, WHEN EVERY PERSON, REGARDLESS OF AGE, CONTINUED TO ENGAGE IN PURPOSEFUL LIVING.....

[1] "Social Security." History. Web. June 2016.

QUESTIONS FOR REFLECTION

Think for yourself . . .

What adjectives would you use to describe your current perception of retirement?

Consider the bigger picture . . .

How did governmental actions help shape attitudes toward old age?

Imagine how it could change . . .

How can your congregation intentionally respect and honor the process of getting older?

CHAPTER 2

Having Anticipatory Vision

Since we cannot change reality, let us change the eyes which see reality.
~Nikos Kazantzakis

Vision is a mental picture of a preferred *future*. Ironically, the construction of vision is most often a past to present based process. It typically engages persons in an assessment of a current reality that is further shaped by past experiences.

Discerning a vision for ministry with the sixty-five and older population of the *future* requires a shift in the visioning approach. We must have strategic anticipation or *anticipatory vision*.

Those who train secret service personnel note that anticipatory vision requires:

1. Seeing the peripheral
2. Seeing the unexpected
3. Identifying the suspicious and unusual activity
4. Imagining possibilities

One of the challenges for the church today is to engage in a strategic *anticipation* of ministry that is needed when the Baby Boomer birth cohort (those born from 1946-1964), becomes a critical mass within the older population. The Baby Boomer's life cycle has, since adolescence, initiated change.

Some of the movements in local church ministry that resulted from their presence included:

- Organized youth ministry, both in local churches and parachurch organizations, as Baby Boomers moved through adolescence
- The contemporary style of worship music and worship teams emerged during Baby Boomer's young adult years
- The type and quality of children's ministry was enhanced, birth through age twelve, as the Baby Boomer cohort became parents

In the best case scenario, Baby Boomers, as a critical mass in the sixty-five and over population in our churches, will transform the approach to "older adult" ministries. In the worst case scenario, they will just ignore these ministries and disengage with the church.

As church leaders create a mental model of this future "older adults" ministry, it's important to identify the potential number and general characteristics of those who might serve and be served. A starting point is to reflect on the current demographics of a congregation.

Consider the Trailing Edge Baby Boomers, born in 1952-1964. Who are they? What are the life transitions they are experiencing? How are they engaged in service?

Next, consider the subgroups within your sixty-five and over population. Various researchers have indicated different levels of aging. The chart below reflects a blending of their theories.

"New" Old	**Age 65-69**
"Young" Old	**Ages 70-74**
"Middle" Old	**Ages 75-79**
Old	**Ages 80-84**
"Oldest" Old	**Ages 85+**

Ask yourself:

1. Which age group makes up the greater percentage of your church?
2. What are the characteristics of each of the subgroups?
3. What are the needs of each subgroup?

Your church exists within a community of concern. Each local church has the responsibility of defining the boundaries of that community.

Facts about the population in your community are easily accessible through online and print resources with data from the U.S. Census Bureau. A listing of options for research is available in the resource section at the back of this book. Some of the demographics to consider are: percentages of persons in various age groups, gender, racial, and ethnic backgrounds, marital status, educational level, and median income levels. In addition to reflecting on your local church and community demographics, one should also consider the general trends emerging across the nation.

~~~~

Longevity[1]

The old in the United States are living longer!

- Life expectancy in 1900: forty-seven
- Life expectancy in 2010: seventy-eight
- In 2015, a male turning age sixty-five could expect to live nineteen more years; a female could expect to live twenty-one more years
- In 2015, one out of every four sixty-five year olds was projected to live past the age of ninety; one out of every ten was expected to live past ninety-five

Density

The United States population is getting older!

- The sixty-five and over population is growing by up to 10,000 people a day since the Baby Boomers began turning sixty-five in 2011; this trend will continue through 2029
- The sixty-five and over population is projected to increase from about 14% of the total population in 2015 to 20% in 2030 and more beyond

---

[1] *Ortman, Jennifer M., Victoria A. Velkoff, and Howard Hogan. "An Aging Nation: The Older Population in the United States." U.S. Census Bureau, May 2014. Web. June 2016., Cited statistics under "Longevity," "Density," and "Diversity." Subsections of chapter.*
~~~~

- 2056 is the projected tipping point, when the percentage of sixty-five and over population will outnumber those under eighteen; the "new old" will be the Millennials, who begin turning sixty-five in 2046

Diversity

The United States is becoming a plurality nation!

- In 2043, it is projected that the non-Hispanic white population will not be a majority in the total population
- The diversity of the older population (sixty-five and over) by 2060 according to 2012 projections from the 2010 U.S. Census will be:
    - Non-Hispanic white – 56%
    - Hispanic – 21.2%
    - Black – 12.5%
    - Asian – 9%
    - Other races (Native American, Alaskan Native, Pacific Islander and Hawaiian, and more than one race) – 1.3%

Ask yourself:

1. Which of these trends are currently influencing your church and community?
2. Which of these trends may be influences in the future?

With the increasing racial and ethnic diversity of the older population, diverse expectations will shape the nature of eldercare as well as needed services within our churches and communities. African American and Hispanic communities have historically viewed the responsibility of care for the older adults to be a family responsibility, with the younger generations caring for older generations.

The concept of caring for older generations in families has eroded some in recent years, given mobility and the increasing number of low-income households within both of these communities. Mobility, both voluntary and involuntary, has had the side effect, for some, of weakening the family bonds and the sense of neighborhood.

MOBILITY, BOTH VOLUNTARY AND INVOLUNTARY, HAS HAD THE SIDE EFFECT, FOR SOME, OF WEAKENING THE FAMILY BONDS AND THE SENSE OF NEIGHBORHOOD.

Lower income levels create additional pressures for both those who give and receive care. The option of paying for outside services isn't available to all who need care. Within the Asian and Native American contexts, the traditional assumption is that older relatives are to be cared for by the young, even if children and grandchildren are living at a distance. Yet, the stresses created by caregiving, both those in close proximity and those at a distance, are becoming more difficult for caregivers to manage. Support for caregivers is now a key issue in many circles.

What does all of this mean for the church? As the late church consultant, Lyle Schaller, once wisely said, "The one thing that you know about the future is that you don't know." Nonetheless, Schaller modeled a practice of mining demographics to engage in strategic anticipatory vision and create innovative models of church ministries for the future.

If we are to take the statistics seriously, we know we are not creating a small tangential ministry for a few older people. **We are visioning and planning for a strategic initiative to connect with the projected largest segment of the population.**

QUESTIONS FOR REFLECTION

Think for yourself . . .

What are you personally experiencing in terms of the increasing sixty-five and over population in your community?

Consider the bigger picture . . .

What serves as a basis of planning for older adult ministries in your church?

Imagine how it could change . . .

How might having strategic anticipation of the "new old" alter your church's approach to older adult ministries?

CHAPTER 3

Preparing For the Future

Old age is like everything else; to make a success of it you have to start young.
~Unknown

Just as it is important to develop plans within a family, workplace, community organization, or church, planning is part of the preparation for the anticipated future in the last phase of life.

The Book of Proverbs has wisdom for here and now, but also for focusing on the future. Many proverbs offer wisdom on how to make plans, why to make them, and what to expect with the best plans we make.

Without counsel plans fail, but with many advisers they succeed.
(Proverbs 15:22 ESV)
Commit your work to the Lord, and your plans will be established.
(Proverbs 16:3 ESV)

Using just these two proverbs—among many addressing how to lay out our futures—we are pointed toward preparing for the future through planning. As Paul Tournier wrote in *"Learn to Grow Old":*

> *"Your manner of life now is already determining your life in the years of old age. This happens without your realizing it and perhaps you are not giving enough thought to it. Therefore, one must prepare oneself for retirement."*

We previously mentioned Caleb from the Book of Joshua in the Bible. At one point while in the Promised Land he exclaimed "So, here I am today, eighty-five years old...." However, Caleb was just forty when he and Joshua returned with their positive words about the Promised Land! What might Caleb have done during those forty-five years between that initial experience and the fulfillment of the promise to occupy his portion of the Promised Land?

The Bible doesn't give us specific information about that time in between, but—based on the outcome, there are some things we can speculate. His faith was strong, so he likely participated in *spiritual growth*. He had followers, so he must have experienced *leadership development*. Caleb was led and led others, so it's probable that he had *mentoring* as both the giver and the receiver. Through all of these efforts, he would have had to *cultivate relationships*.

There are some words that might characterize Caleb; these words can give us a sense of direction in our own preparation efforts.

- **Vision**—Caleb had a clear picture of God's preferred future
- **Vitality**—Caleb possessed energy, vitality, and optimism
- **Vigor**—Caleb maintained his physical health, healthy interactions with others, spiritual disciplines, and perseverance
- **Victory**—Caleb planned, prepared for, and implemented the vision he was given by God. **Forty-five *years* of planning and preparation went into one *moment* of promise**

> CALEB PLANNED, PREPARED FOR, AND IMPLEMENTED THE VISION HE WAS GIVEN BY GOD.

~~~~

As Paul Tournier said, "Start giving thought to preparing." The moment of promise awaits!

ATTITUDE ADJUSTMENT

In 1961, authors Elaine Cumming and Warren Early Henry asserted the "disengagement theory" in their book, *"Growing Old".* The theory not only claimed that the elderly should systematically withdraw from the social roles of their younger years, due to the inevitability of death; it actually
~~~~

encouraged society at large to mutually recognize that they will one day have to function without those older adults and, therefore, withdrawal is both acceptable and normal.

The disengagement theory was considered invalid in the 1970s and yet the principles within it seem to be influencing many older adults today, as well as continuing to shape the attitudes of younger generations.

The *attitudes* about aging which were formed earlier in life, have the power to shape *expectations* and can ultimately create the *roles* that a person assumes in the last phase of life. Misperceptions of aging tend to form doubts about the ability of the older population to function productively in society.

THE ATTITUDES ABOUT AGING WHICH WERE FORMED EARLIER IN LIFE, HAVE THE POWER TO SHAPE EXPECTATIONS AND CAN ULTIMATELY CREATE THE ROLES THAT A PERSON ASSUMES IN THE LAST PHASE OF LIFE.

One's attitudes can shape actions resulting in denial of our own aging process and create barriers that can exclude many older adults from engaging in *the whole of life*.

We need to be reeducated through learning truth rather than accepting myths. Amy Hanson in her book, "*Baby Boomers and Beyond*", identifies common myths about older adults. Some of the myths suggested by her are further described here. They include an inability to adapt to change, an expected loss of memory, a reduced capacity to learn, default increases in spirituality, and a non-societal contributive use of time.

ADAPTABILITY TO CHANGE

It is a myth that older adults are unable to adapt to change.

The truth is that research[1] shows that there is *no* strong correlation between age and our ability to change. Adapting to change when older has more to do with how we have dealt with changes earlier in life and whether we have learned to manage transitions effectively.

LOSS OF MEMORY

It is a myth that all older adults experience significant memory loss.

The truth is that studies indicate fewer than fifteen percent of persons sixty-five and older experience significant memory loss[2]. Alzheimer's is a *disease,* not a normal part of the aging process. As one grows older, thinking processes may slow down and it can take longer to retrieve short-term memory. However, memory loss overall is not a characteristic of the normal aging process.

---

[1] *Andrew J. Martin, Harry Nejad, Susan Colmar and Gregory Arief D. Liem (2012). Adaptability: Conceptual and Empirical Perspectives on Responses to Change, Novelty and Uncertainty. Australian Journal of Guidance and Counselling, 22, pp 58-81. doi:10.1017/jgc.2012.8.*

[2] *2016 Alzheimer's Disease Facts and Figures, a statistical resource for U.S. data related to Alzheimer's disease, the most common cause of dementia, as well as other dementias, by Alzheimer's Association*

CAPACITY TO LEARN

It is a myth that older adults are unable to learn new information.

The truth is that studies[1] indicate that we can learn and grow until the very end of our lives. Learning environments and motivation must be given special attention. Changes in vision and hearing will require adaptations. Topics addressing felt needs will motivate participation such as using computers and smart phones to stay in touch with grandchildren. Surveys indicate forty-three percent of Americans over age sixty-five are on social media[2].

INCREASED SPIRITUALITY

It is a myth that older adults tend to become more spiritual as they age.

The truth is that results from the Barna study in 2014[3] noted forty-three percent of the total United States population is unchurched and within that group forty-nine percent are Baby Boomers and persons sixty-five and over. The same studies indicate that older adults (born 1945 and earlier) have the greatest percentage in attendance of any

---

[1] *"Brain and Behavior Are Modifiable, Even as We Get Older." Elsevier Connect. Web. June 2016, Cognitive Plasticity, presented by Ursula Staudinger, PhD, Director of the Robert N. Butler Columbia Aging Center at Columbia University.*

[2] *Brenner, Joanna, and Aaron Smith. "72% of Online Adults Are Social Networking Site Users." Pew Research Center Internet Science Tech RSS. Pew Research Center, 05 Aug. 2013. Web. 6 June 2016*

[3] *Reported in "Churchless: Understanding Today's Unchurched and How to Connect with Them," October 1, 2014, by George Barna (Editor), David Kinnaman (Editor).*

age group in church, but attendance may be from habit and not an indication of allowing God's Word to transform their lives (heart and hand). Intentional evangelism and discipleship are needed.

USE OF TIME

It is a myth that older adults want to spend all of their time relaxing and living a life of leisure.

The truth is that older adults, particularly the new old, desire *to make a difference* with their lives. According to a Bureau of Labor Statistics 2014 report[1] on volunteering, volunteers age sixty-five and over noted forty-three percent did their service mainly through or for a religious organization. This is good news for the church and Christian nonprofits ***if* we can create *meaningful* volunteer opportunities**.

> THE TRUTH IS THAT OLDER ADULTS, PARTICULARLY THE NEW OLD, DESIRE TO MAKE A DIFFERENCE WITH THEIR LIVES.

[1] *"Volunteering in 2014: The Economics Daily: U.S. Bureau of Labor Statistics." U.S. Bureau of Labor Statistics. U.S. Bureau of Labor Statistics, n.d. Web. June 2016.*

EXPLORING IDENTITY

A question that emerges often when entering the last phase of life is *Who am I?* The formation of an identity is a key task in the earlier years of one's life, particularly adolescence and early adulthood. The remainder of one's life provides opportunities to confirm that identity through lived experiences.

Sadly, the nature of one's identity often morphs during middle adult years to align with responses to three questions:

1. **What do I do?**
2. **What do I have?**
3. **What do others say about me?**

Prior to the time of disengagement from the workplace, or the demand of managing a household, one's life is often spent pursuing the ultimate *doing goals* as measured in productivity and reward. A question about doing is often the first question when meeting someone new: *What do you do?*

Imagine the awkward silence or the response of, *not much,* that emerges when that question is asked of a person who has retired, whether at sixty-five or later. Silence or such a seemingly innocent response could, even at a subconscious level on the part of the giver and receiver, unintentionally imply a purposeless existence.

The question about what one has, whether asked by others or of oneself, leads to responses often focused on one's assets.

- Investments?
- Savings?
- Checking Accounts?
- Home?
- Furnishings?
- Car?
- Clothes?
- Technological equipment?

The responses can generate further unsettling personal questions such as *Do I have enough?*

The third question, *What do others say about me?* has considerable power. Who are we when the "doing" attached to the busyness of workplace and family responsibilities is no longer *our* doing and the capacity to increase our "haves" is limited? How will others describe us?

Rather than have one's identity shaped by questions about doing, having, and the thoughts of others, as a Christian, the focus can be on different questions:

1. **"How does God see me?"**
2. **"What is my calling?"**

Ephesians 2:10 (NIV) provides insight to God's vision.

> *"For we are God's handiwork, created in Christ Jesus to do good works, which God prepared in advance for us to do."*

We are God's handiwork, the beloved. As Henri Nouwen noted in his book, *"Life of the Beloved*":

> *"....a person should say to oneself, repeatedly, I am the chosen child of God, precious in God's eyes, called the Beloved from all eternity and held safe in an everlasting embrace."*

God's intention in one's calling is greater than the products and rewards of an occupation. He has entrusted His people with the welfare of the entire human race. Jesus was a carpenter—it was His occupation, or, what He DID—but His real calling was to redeem the world. As Christians we are to continue Christ's work in the world. There is no chronological age at which we are released from the responsibility of advancing Christ's mission!

CLARIFYING PURPOSE

For a Christian, one's calling will not change at its core during the aging process. What may change is the way in which it is lived out while being attentive to the voice of God and the needs of the world.

Each of us is an experiment of one. We can explore and find the right connection between God's calling, our means of serving, and the world around us. As Fredrick Buechner stated, *"The place God calls you to, is the place where your deep gladness and the world's deep hunger meet."* The person who experiences this alignment between occupation and personal gladness is fortunate. Often, however, the calling is lived out in the discretionary time, outside of the occupational workplace.

Max DePree emphasizes this idea in his book, *"Leadership is an Art"*, as he relates the story of his father, CEO at the time, going to visit the family of the just deceased millwright.

> *"My father is the founder of Herman Miller, and much of the value system and impounded energy of the company, a legacy still drawn on today, is part of his contribution. In the furniture industry of the 1920s, the machines of most factories were not run by electric motors, but by pulleys from a central drive shaft. The millwright was the person on whom the entire activity of the operation depended. He was a key person. One day, the millwright died.*
>
> *My father, being a younger manager at the time, did not know what he should do when a key person died, but thought he ought to go visit the family. He went to the house and was invited to join the family in the living room. There was some*

> *awkward conversation—the kind with which many of us are familiar.*
>
> *The widow asked my father if it would be all right if she read aloud some poetry. Naturally, he agreed. She went into another room, came back with a bound book and for many minutes read selected pieces of beautiful poetry. When she finished, my father commented on how beautiful the poetry was and asked who wrote it. She replied that her husband, the millwright, was the poet.*
>
> *In the many years since the millwright died, my father and many of us at Herman Miller continue to wonder. Was he a poet who did millwright's work OR was he a millwright who wrote poetry?"*

Preparation for the future involves exploring and clarifying purpose. For some, it may mean repurposing. Whether articulated for the first time, or adjusted for a new phase of life, having clarity around one's purpose is a necessary first step to one's future preparations. It is important for the individual to have a clear sense of meaning and purpose. Paul Irving, chair of the Center for the Future of Aging notes studies at the Center[1]. Those studies report that purposeful living correlates with longevity. Having a clear sense of purpose in the later years of life promotes physical well-being and motivation for continued learning and

---

[1] *Paul Irving, Purposeful Aging: A Model for a New Life Course, October 2015, at www.milkeninstitute.org/publications/view/760*

serving. Irving notes that purpose can be a buffer to counter the pain and losses which come with aging. He cites *"Man's Search for Meaning"* in which psychiatrist, Victor Frankl, wrote: "Life is never made unbearable by circumstances, but only by lack of meaning and purpose."

LIVING THROUGH TRANSITIONS

Change is an inevitable reality of aging. We have *continual endings* and *numerous new beginnings*. The life we had will not be the same as the life that's in front of us. We must allow God to replace what we've had with new experiences (and sometimes persons) with grateful acknowledgment. As Corrie Ten Boom wrote in "*The Hiding Place*":

> *"This is what the past is for! Every experience God gives us and every person He puts in our lives is the perfect preparation for the future that only He can see."*

William Bridges, a respected theorist in managing transitions, says that *change* (defined as transformation or modification) is situational, while *transition* (defined as movement or passage from one stage to another) is psychological. Bridges describes three transition stages:

The Endings – a time when people need to let go of the past and process the losses

The Neutral Zone – a time when people discern new possibilities and explore their comfort with the next phase

The New Beginnings – a time when people embrace new experiences and a new "normal" for life

These three stages of transition do not have distinct boundaries. While in the Neutral Zone, the ending has not yet been completed and the new beginning is in process of being formed.

> THESE THREE STAGES OF TRANSITION DO NOT HAVE DISTINCT BOUNDARIES.

During the first phase of endings, or processing losses and letting go, it is important to name the real, expected losses. A simple process of reflection and writing down one's perceptions of anticipated loss before such occurs is helpful.

Take a sheet of paper and create three columns with headings:

Things I Will Lose	Things That Will Stay The Same	Things I Will Gain

Just naming the potential losses can prepare one for the actual time when he or she will face a particular loss. Recognizing the things that will stay the same will provide a sense of continuity and stability. Listing things one will gain stimulates feelings of anticipation.

Swiss psychiatrist, Elisabeth Kubler-Ross, introduced the widely accepted five stages of grief after loss including: denial, anger, bargaining, depression and acceptance. These stages of grief may all be experienced as losses and are processed during the Endings. During the process of grieving, though, we must remember that the five stages are not stops on a linear timeline. There may be a recycling of old feelings again and again as we retreat to the past and try to hang on to the familiar.

Transition is a unique time of being caught between memory and hope. The key to living effectively and joyfully through transition is to keep moving toward the new beginning. The Neutral Zone is an in-between time, but it is not merely a waiting room between the past and the future. During this phase of transition, we may experience feelings of disorientation and ambiguity. Questions such as *Who am I?* and *What is my purpose?* should not become barriers, but rather they should serve as platforms for creative exploration.

The Neutral Zone is a time for personal research and development to create the future. We can experiment with new areas for serving, learning, and relationships. This creative approach helps the process of A) discerning purpose in the next phase of life, and B) creating a mental picture of a desired future.

We do not wake up one day and see a digital sign saying *This is the New Beginning.* Instead, during the Neutral Zone—when the endings are still being processed—the new beginning is gradually formed. First, one must have clarity in purpose, then a mental picture envisioned for the future, and lastly a road map created for actual participation in that future.

Throughout the entire process of forming a new beginning, prayer is needed. Yes, we must trust the process, but we must also trust God *in* the process. The new beginning emerges slowly, but at some point it is important to have a symbolic experience that signals the reality of the old being released and the new beginning embraced.

How one is able to manage transitions in earlier years of life often correlates with the ability to adapt to changes and live effectively and joyfully through the transitions in the later stages of life. Many changes occur earlier in life such as: leaving one's childhood home, marriage or the choice to stay single, relocating, moving, having children, adopting, or choosing not to have children, becoming empty nesters, having grandchildren, starting or changing careers, death of close relatives and friends, and other events that require life alterations. Whether it is an involuntary or voluntary change that one experiences, there is a transition time to process endings, as well as create and embrace new beginnings.

Living through transition is like being a trapeze artist. One must let go of the first trapeze bar (endings), fly through the empty space (neutral zone), and then grab hold of the next bar (new beginnings). Flying in emptiness is not a very comfortable place and people often want to rush through this in-between time rather than engage in processing the endings, creative exploration, and risk-taking of new beginnings. Some key principles to remember in the three stages of transition are:

- Offer gratitude to God for the persons and experiences He has provided in the past
- Offer prayers of lament for the crises and difficult experiences
- Express thanksgiving to those who have shared in your journey
- Remind yourself this is a time of reorienting and redefining, not meaningless waiting
- Limit additional changes as much as possible; don't undergo multiple transitions if you have a choice
- Expect to feel some uncomfortable emotions such as fear, anger, or guilt
- Set short-term, achievable goals, so you have a sense of movement forward while you are on the path toward your long-term goals
- Explore your gifts and passions to discern potential engagements in learning, service, and meaningful leisure and social activities
- Cultivate both old and new friendships to recognize your lasting close relationships

During transitions, it is valuable to establish accountability, either through writing and reflecting, or by partnering with a friend or small group to do a regular check-in with regard to progress. Again, staying in the process is key. The more one engages in transition, the more he or she will feel confident in knowing that the trapeze bar on the other side *will* be there.

QUESTIONS FOR REFLECTION

Think about yourself...

What is important to you personally about the topics explored in this chapter?

Attitude adjustment –

Exploring identity –

Clarifying purpose –

Living through transitions -

Consider the bigger picture . . .

What is the next level of thinking you need to do in each of these areas?

Imagine how it could change . . .

Which of these topics, if any, need immediate attention in your church?

CHAPTER 4

Living Vital Lives

The best way to predict the future is to invent it.

~Peter Drucker

We are all aging. Each morning, when one wakes, a person is one day older. The message from Baby Boomers is often that they don't *want* to think about getting older. The exponential increase in anti-aging products and media messages about what constitutes vibrant living validates this message. As a birth cohort, the Baby Boomers have been change agents throughout their lives, creating new approaches for many aspects of life.

The one thing that this large birth cohort in United States history cannot change, though, is the reality that upon waking each morning a person is one day older. What can change, however, are the attitudes we have toward growing older and the approaches we take to live vitally in this next phase of life. Just as the Boomers initiated movements to dismantle sexism and racism, they can initiate the dismantling of ageism. We need these change agents! They can help dispel the myths and counter the negative perceptions of older adults. In doing so, they will help their own generation and generations to follow. They will also help many in their late sixties, seventies, and beyond who reject the ageist stereotypes.

One of the most effective ways to dismantle an ageist system is through increasing awareness of persons who have lived or are living **vital lives** (actively engaged lives of contribution to society through their gifts) all the days of their lives. The power of their stories can help persons unlearn early-formed negative attitudes, relearn expectations, and embrace roles based on new, positive thoughts and actions.

As Winston Churchill stated: "Attitude is a little thing that makes a big difference." How a person thinks and feels in relation to growing old will make a difference in the behaviors exemplified when a person is old. That attitude will be a determiner of whether the last phase of life is "a nonlife or a new life" as author Joan Chittister describes in "*The Gift of Years.*" That attitude will determine whether the last phase of life is as full as the earlier phases of life – whether it is a "VITAL LIFE."

~~~~
~~~~

VitaLives

ISABELLE

Isabelle lived to be 103. Her last twenty-five years were spent as a widow living in a retirement community. That time was the beginning of a new era. Isabelle transitioned from being a long-time pastor's wife to living on her own, albeit in a continuing care retirement center.

- *She started a group which recycled old greeting cards into new ones.*
- *She hosted coffee hours for her section of the campus and co-chaired the all-campus bazaar.*

On Isabelle's 100th birthday, she was headed to the airport in a taxi. The retirement center workers and fellow residents asked, "Are you going by yourself?"

Her reply was simply, "No, there will be a whole plane full of people."

HILDEGARD

Hildegard married for the first time at age sixty-seven, several years after retiring from a public school teaching career. Early in her retirement she discerned that the church leaders had "put her on a shelf." Some of the roles she had assumed just disappeared without her agreement. In response several years later, she commented, "I'm going to come off that shelf and get involved."

Get involved she did!

- Hildegard continued engagement in teaching and creative arts, both in her church and in her community.
- She mentored younger leaders until her death at age ninety-five.
- She was a great eraser of generational divides, reaching out to all generations and using her God-given gifts with all ages.

Hildegard boldly and shamelessly defied ageist stereotypes. The negative generalizations about age would have shelved Hildegard nearly thirty years before she was done giving back. Countless would have lost out on her many contributions.

~~~~

The lessons learned from Isabelle and Hildegard left ripple effects that continue to shape many lives today. The
~~~~

manner in which they lived their lives demonstrates a legacy that, in humility, each would have noted as simply *living out God's call all the days of their lives.*

Isabelle and Hildegard maintained physical and mental well-being all the days of their lives. This is not always the nature of the journey. Aging can bring declines in both physical and cognitive functioning. Life for some just gets harder. Acceptance of these realities is the key to continuing on a path of vital living.

PHIL

Consider the vital life of Phil. Over a period of twenty-two years prior to his death at age eighty-three, Phil experienced many physical changes that reduced his mobility. The onset of these issues led to his retirement at age sixty-one. He then learned new ways to be "at work," tapping into his creativity through painting, counted cross-stitch, and cooking. The products of his "work" became gifts to express his care for others. With the onset of non-treatable macular degeneration, Phil had to adjust, but he didn't stop engaging!

He became more active with cooking and baking, often for large groups. Using a low vision magnifier, he managed household finances, read daily, used word search books, and prepared his memoirs, over 150 *handwritten* pages, as a gift for his children and grandchildren. Through intercessory prayer and presence via phone contact, he continued caring for others.

Phil's acceptance of physical challenges opened the way for vital living all the days of his life.

BOB

Bob had to address acceptance when his wife of sixty-eight years, Muriel, began to show signs of dementia. He was determined to care for her at home and did so for nearly nine years after those early signs. Initially, Bob tried to have her do as much as she could for herself. He took Muriel to church where she was able to sing the hymns and recite the Lord's Prayer. Those outings also provided opportunities for socialization. He extended the efforts of social stimulation by welcoming visitors to their home.

When it came to the point that caring for his wife at home was an impossible task for him to do on his own, they moved *together* into a continuing care retirement center. Muriel was in the skilled nursing area and Bob resided in independent living. He was able to walk and visit her every day and also interact with the other residents. She received excellent care and showed occasional signs of recognition. He stayed active and was pleased to be in such proximity.

Initially, Bob felt some loss at giving up his house and the chores he enjoyed. However, he soon came to enjoy the freedom of his new life, and he was able to find comfort in visiting Muriel, going to church, and interacting with others.

~~~~
~~~~

Change and related losses will happen to us, as well as to those around us. Acceptance of change releases everything to be what it already is and allows the new to emerge for continued vital living.

> CHANGE AND RELATED LOSSES WILL HAPPEN TO US, AS WELL AS TO THOSE AROUND US.

Finding older adults living VITAL LIVES today is not difficult. Many are within our families, among our work colleagues, in our neighborhoods, in community organizations, and our churches. The stories that follow are a few of the persons who have modeled vital living for us and who, through their lives, have left us with words of wisdom.

~~~~

LENORE

Once the decision was made to retire at age sixty, Lenore engaged in a process that moved swiftly. During a single week, she left her job and colleagues, moved to a new home, and flew to Canada to attend a symposium for a Master of Arts Intercultural Studies (MAIS) program with the North American Institute of Indigenous Theological Studies. Lenore wasn't finishing; she was just beginning! During those years since all of her changes, Lenore has engaged as a part-time graduate student, a commissioner on the Washington State Human Rights Commission, a facilitator of Journey to Mosaic (a reconciliation and justice ministry of her regional
~~~~

conference, Pacific Northwest), and a member of various boards serving both her Native American community and her church.

Lenore cites the two major contributors to maintaining a vital life as: 1) her two *takojas* (Lakota for grandchildren) for whom she is a part-time caregiver, and 2) returning to graduate school to open doors to new seasons of life. She notes the takojas are "life bringers" and the graduate studies respond to her yearning to follow Jesus as a Lakota woman, having almost always been the only Native American in a predominantly white church. One hope Lenore has for the future is to find ways to apply all that Jesus is forming in her, so that she can help offer new life in the economically depressed neighborhood being served by the church plant she is helping to start.

Lenore's words of wisdom for those in their fifties and sixties looking toward the next phase of life:

"...plan for retirement and ask Jesus to walk you into it. In my case, the opportunity and timing arose at the prompting of my son's family, and once I said 'yes,' I recognized that all events were falling into place. Watch for the circumstances that Jesus offers to move you along. Retirement is actually life giving!"

WILL

Will recently stepped aside at age sixty-six from full-time employment as a vice president in an engineering firm. He has entered a phased retirement. At this time, Will continues to work full-time as an independent contractor completing some hold over projects. His intent is to decrease time as projects are completed. Will believes his leadership experience and gifts in both independent consulting and related ministry opportunities will contribute to living a vital life in this next phase. His hope for the future is to continue to lead a productive and relevant life-style that is guided by interests and passions, not limited by professional requirements.

Will's words of wisdom for persons in their fifties and sixties looking toward the next phase of life:

"Work with a financial advisor to be prepared for the next phase. Create and continually update a next phase plan. I used a framework from an article on planning and created my own spreadsheet to identify hopes and dreams for each area of my life."

JIM

Jim looks back at the six years after his decision (at age sixty-four) to step aside from a full-time pastoral role, and he sees how God has used his experiences and education to prepare him for a vital life after retirement. During those six years, Jim embraced an encore career as a spiritual director, offering individual spiritual direction, supervision of spiritual directors, and leadership for retreats. His administrative gifts have been used extensively in his role as coordinator of a regional pastoral spiritual director network, president pro-tem of a newly formed denominational association of spiritual directors, coordinator of *Sustaining Pastoral Excellence* retreats, and co-leader of a local clergy fellowship. Jim has served as adjunct faculty at Mercy Center in the Bay Area for two programs equipping persons to serve as spiritual directors. The freedom to choose how he invests his time has opened the way for more extensive engagement in his community through involvement with a variety of programs focused on improving the lives of children and youth.

Jim cites three major contributors in his preretirement years to preparing for continued vital living including: 1) meetings with a spiritual director which ultimately led to training and practice as a spiritual director, 2) engagement in community service organizations while serving as pastor, and 3) a discovery in his mid-fifties that cycling was the most enjoyable exercise for him which could be continued in retirement.

One hope Jim has for his future is that he can remain open to a healthy rhythm of life (spiritual, physical, intellectual, emotional, and social). He also hopes to continue to grow into whatever new ministries God invites him into and work as a partner in His Kingdom.

Jim's words of wisdom for persons in their fifties and sixties looking toward the next phase of life:

"Prepare during your last years of the full-time occupation for activities full of meaning in your retirement. It may be something new and different than you've done, or it may be a continuation of one or two of the most enjoyable aspects of what you have been doing for years."

SHARON S.

Sharon looks forward to a second encore career in the beginning years of her seventh decade of life. Her first encore career began when she stepped aside from full-time compensated employment at the age of sixty-one. During the ten years since that decision, Sharon completed life and leadership coach training, taught at a nearby university, and developed the curriculum for several leadership courses in their school of professional studies. She also served as the part-time Life Groups pastor at a church plant. Sharon believes completing her bachelor's degree and master's degree as an adult student paved the way for teaching and working with adults in the church and teaching university classes. In addition she notes her connection with the Evangelical Covenant Church nearly forty years ago and related involvements through Christian education ministry in the regional conference have shaped relationships and experiences beyond retirement.

Sharon's primary hope for the future is to continue to use her gifts, be an encourager, and challenge, inspire, and guide those who God leads to her so they recognize and reach their full God-given potential. Sharon also hopes to be more generous with her time, talent, and treasure beyond her full-time working years.

Sharon's words of wisdom for persons in their fifties and sixties looking toward the next phase of life:

"Focus on your strengths; keep learning and growing; let go of habits, patterns, and expectations that aren't serving you well in this season; and trust God in the midst of it all! The best is yet to come! Put relationships first!"

JORGE

Jorge, a scholar and teacher during his career, continues pursuing these passions at age seventy-two. After retiring at age sixty-four as president of *Centro Hispano Estudios Teologicos* (CHET), a theological school for Latinos in California, he and his wife entered an encore career. They prepared for and served as short-term Covenant missionaries for five years in Spain. After concluding service as missionaries and returning to the United States, Jorge continued to teach and preach at churches and retreats, serve as pastoral counselor in his own church, teach at several theological seminaries, and review and update the digitized textbooks and manuals for training of lay pastoral counselors. These books and manuals are used in several Spanish-speaking countries and in courses at CHET.

Jorge's life experiences and education have all contributed to his post-retirement passions and engagements. His experience also helped him in caring for his wife who has a declining memory. In the future, Jorge's hope is to keep serving his Lord and His people.

Jorge's words of wisdom for persons in their fifties and sixties looking toward the next phase of life:

"Prepare for many changes and adjustments. Be flexible. Keep the joy of your salvation. Demonstrate gratitude and generosity on a daily basis. Have a purpose or project in which you invest your time. Exercise physically as much as possible. Cultivate your relationships with family and friends."

SHARON D.

Since leaving full-time employment at the age of sixty-four, Sharon has engaged in holistic community development work in Cameroon as a Covenant short-term missionary.

Currently, she is engaged in community development work through her home church, Oakdale Covenant Church, in Chicago, Illinois. She continues to be a consultant to the leaders she trained in holistic community development in Camaroon and travels to Camaroon twice a year. Sharon believes a major contributor to her approach to post-retirement years was her family's example (persons from four generations) of continuing to "work" after they retired from "real" work. They modeled living with the conviction that while on this earth you have to "pay rent" and help your neighbors. Sharon's dream, now at age seventy-two, is to move to a farm where people living in urban communities can come and learn about the value of the land, the value of collective work, healthy eating, how to cook and preserve foods, and heal from the trauma of life in the urban communities.

Sharon's words of wisdom for persons in their fifties and sixties looking toward the next phase of life:

"Life is not ending--it's just beginning. Dream big dreams."

As with all of those who inspire us with their vital lives, Sharon continues to grow toward God by serving His Kingdom and His purpose for her life. To watch a video testimonial about Sharon's vital life, scan the code at the right or visit: https://youtu.be/GsC25GYt8zQ.

ALLAN AND JOYCE

Allan and Joyce embraced new beginnings at age sixty when they stepped aside from full-time employment and moved 2100 miles across the country to join in planting a new church. Allan first served as the "interim" business manager for the regional conference of churches, Pacific Southwest, while he and Joyce helped start a new church plant in Santa Barbara. Allan continued to provide excellence in business management for the church plant for over a decade. His financial expertise and ministry focus assisted a local foundation, the regional conference, and two regional Christian camps. Allan credits being a part of the regional conference ministry and working with church plants for redirecting the lives of both he and his wife. This involvement was enhanced with meeting and making friends from many different countries in their new community. A hope for the future expressed by Allan and Joyce, now in their late seventies, is to continue providing enthusiasm and leadership for existing and new innovative programs where they live in Samarkand, a Covenant Retirement Community, in Santa Barbara.

Allan and Joyce's words of wisdom for persons in their fifties and sixties looking toward the next phase of life:

"When the opportunity is there, take advantage and put your whole being into it."

STANLEY

Stanley stepped aside from full-time ministry as a local church pastor when he was seventy-three. During the past five years he has engaged in a wide range of ministries with a new freedom to determine his own daily schedule. Included among those engagements are: serving as a board chair for a foundation seeking to impact the lives of those most in need and a national non-profit board that strengthens local churches by promoting excellence in leadership, consulting for a Christian publishing house, starting his own coaching ministry, serving as an associate trainer with Equip Ministries to train leaders in the Caribbean, taking people on spiritual and educational tours around the world, and being available to mentor younger leaders.

Stanley believes living a vital life in these "retirement" years has been shaped earlier in his life by serving people, continuous learning through reading or travel, and walking with God wherever He leads. He notes being able to say "no, I don't feel like doing that is wonderful" and being free to go or stay is a wonderful liberty that retirement provides. His hope for the future is to be able to stay healthy so he can continue to contribute!

> BEING FREE TO GO OR STAY IS A WONDERFUL LIBERTY THAT RETIREMENT PROVIDES.

Stanley's words of wisdom for persons in their fifties and sixties looking toward the next phase of life:

"Plan what you are going to do when you retire and set in motion what needs to be in place to enjoy that phase of life. It's more than just money!"

PAUL

Paul retired at age sixty-five from service as a denominational president, a role he assumed after many years as a local church pastor. In post-retirement years, his passion to reach the unreached with the Gospel and love for all of God's children intersected with education and experience as he chaired the beginning phases of two foundations for India: The William Carey Heritage Foundation and Truth Seekers International. At the same time he was a lay leader in a new church plant, engaged as a volunteer at a juvenile detention center, and served as an adjunct professor at three seminaries. Paul notes that significant contributors, to his living a vital life, have been a Godly and caring wife, a promising pension plan, good health, and a wealth of great, honest friends in both high and low times. At the age of eighty-two, Paul's hope for his future is to finish well which includes securing the best both spiritually and financially for his family, writing his autobiography, and completing his foundation work as an officer and director.

Paul's words of wisdom for persons in their fifties and sixties looking toward the next phase of life:

"Invest emotionally and physically in serving others—but not as a professional. Make sure you have not blurred the distinction between your office, career, and successes with a joyous and active identity when you step down and 'refire.' Seek to end well with courage, gentleness, and love."

ROD

Rod stepped aside from compensated employment at age eighty-four when he and his wife moved to Covenant Retirement Community in Turlock, California. Although this new season of being apart from employment is only eighteen months, his vital life has not "missed a beat." Rod continues to serve as a preacher and teacher -- providing pulpit supply in his own and surrounding churches, substituting for teachers in Bible classes, and speaking in chapel at the retirement community. In addition he leads workshops at conferences on older adult ministry. He notes that his prior experience in a wide range of ministry responsibilities and periodic changes in location and positions has provided a sense of continuity for his life purpose during this transition. Rod's one hope is to continue ministry through preaching, teaching, and assisting churches with older adult ministries until he dies. During recent years, there have been physical challenges, but Rod's identity as God's child created for His good works provides the motivation to continue "running the race."

> **Rod's words of wisdom for persons in their fifties and sixties looking toward the next phase of life:**

"Plan early for retirement to continue ministry. Set goals for the rest of your life. Plan to move to a Covenant Retirement Community (or similar setting). Make end of life plans."

~~~~

We encourage you to gather your own Vital Life stories. Engage in dialogue with older persons modeling vital living and learn from them.

Recently, in a dialogue with seventy-seven year old Marv, he responded to the question, "What keeps you excited about the future and your calling in ministry?"

> *"Our pastor encourages us and tells us we're not too old, and we can still take risks and do something for the Kingdom. And I believe that!*
>
> *I commit myself to prayer, and as I pray for others I feel engaged in what they're doing. I ride my bike with purpose as I want to be ready physically if and when He may open the door for me to be in active ministry again.*
~~~~

I keep in touch with key people I've had a relationship with for years. These "Young Lions of Judah" make me feel strong as I watch and listen and pray for them as they work in the Kingdom.

I read and journal and pray, sometimes almost as an exercise of discipline, but I press on. And at times there comes a light of Joy!

And when a possibility for further engagement in direct ministry comes along I make myself available.

The adventure of following Him goes on! Even at seventy-seven, I like it!"

Marv's adventure does continue to go on and on as, not long after he spoke these words, he accepted an interim position as pastor of an international ministry in Hong Kong.

~~~~

The vitality of older persons is not a recent phenomenon. Some of the greatest achievers in recent centuries were older persons engaged in vital living. When accomplishments big and small are recognized without regard for assignment to age, we—as a society—can begin the work of removing our expectations of limitations.

- Nelson Mandela, at age seventy-six, was elected president of South Africa
~~~~

- Mother Theresa established the "Missionaries of Charity" order of nuns when she was forty and was awarded the Nobel Peace Prize when she was sixty-nine
- Anna Mary (Grandma) Robertson Moses first picked up a paintbrush when she was seventy-six, but her paintings are sensations in New York, Vienna, and Paris

Hope is stronger than memory.

Now faith is being sure of what we hope for and certain of what we do not see.

(Hebrews 11:1 NIV)

Hope as a noun is an attitude of the mind based upon the expectation of positive outcomes. Hope as a verb is to expect with confidence.

Hope is the very conviction that led Hildegard to "come off the shelf" despite what those around her were subtly communicating. She accepted the reality of change, transitioned effectively, and initiated new beginnings for a life of significance during her remaining twenty-eight years. It's a life of significance that emerges from each of these Vital Life stories.

QUESTIONS FOR REFLECTION

Think about yourself . . .

What learnings have you gained from the vital lives of older adults in your life?

Consider the bigger picture . . .

Who are the older adults living vital lives with whom you interact today? What are you learning?

Imagine how it could change . . .

How can your church highlight the stories of their older adults living vital lives?

IN SUMMARY....

Ageism is another "ism" such as sexism and racism that continues to infiltrate our society and even our churches. A looming factor here is that ageism can be externally imposed or may be a product of one's own denial. As with any "ism" personal experience and relationships are necessary to overcome faulty perceptions.

The Bible speaks of our journey with God not ending here on earth until we draw our last breath. Living fully until we die is God's plan for our lives. There are numerous scriptures depicting the benefits of growing old and staying faithful.

> LIVING FULLY UNTIL WE DIE IS GOD'S PLAN FOR OUR LIVES.

Recently someone said, and it has probably been said many times, that getting older can be difficult, but dying young is a poor alternative. Even though there are often burdens involved in the aging process, there is also the opportunity to make choices about generous living and giving and there are some amazing benefits to aging:

- There is accumulated wisdom
- There may be resources to share
- There is time to give
- Mentoring opportunities abound

It is clear that getting older is a process. Most people have experienced childhood and adolescence. Many have also seen life as a young or middle-aged adult; but, many of you have not been old.

A large number of people are experiencing later years and increasing numbers are on the precipice of those experiences. In order for the later years of life to be significant, planning, preparation, and practice are required. These ideas have all been mentioned.

What has to be reiterated is that one size does not fit all. There is no single right way. Each person approaches aging differently. Each congregation should tailor ministry by, with, and for older adults based on their own internal and external demographics.

According to gerontologists, sociologists and psychologists there are many stages of aging, including:

- New old
- Young old
- Middle old
- Old
- Oldest old

Each stage of aging will have differing wants, needs, and interests.

The same principle runs as a thread through the many cultures in our increasingly diverse country. The challenges of maintaining the worth and dignity of all, regardless of age, are common. Perceptions of the responsibility for caring for older adults do have variances among African American, Asian, Hispanic, Native American, Alaskan Native, Hawaiian Native, Pacific Islander, and White communities. We can learn from one another.

The overarching concept presented in the preparation guide provided here (and lived through so many vital life stories shared) is that we must raise awareness. We have to define reality. The changing demographics are influencing our society and affecting our churches. It is a new day and the characteristics of older adults will continue to change. Ministry by, with and for an aging population is more than potlucks and personal care. It is about valuing and celebrating life. It is about what God can do through committed people. Churches have the opportunity to lead the way and not default by reacting.

God can and will use us at any age. There is no age limit on the way He works. The time is right and the need is great to continue serving God by honoring, encouraging, preparing and equipping God's people to love and serve the body of Christ and the communities around us. This applies to people of all ages and especially for those whom God has gifted with longevity.

PART II
PLAN TO SERVE OTHERS

Enough talk. Now, let's make a difference in someone else's life today. Let's go serve somebody.

~Dave Workman

CHAPTER 5

A Framework for Planning

Old age is not old until regrets take the place of dreams.

~Unknown

You *can* do anything, but you *can't* do everything. Making wise choices for investment of resources—specifically time and money—is essential in planning older adult ministries. The desired outcome of those ministries is to further the ongoing growth of older adults to be like the tree described in Psalm 1:3 (NIV).

> *That person is like a tree planted by streams of water, which yields its fruit in season and whose leaf does not wither—whatever they do prospers.*

It is the sum of all we do that matters. The past influences the present, which helps us to prepare for the future. We often talk about the quantity of life – a number that, as we've addressed, has significantly increased over the past century, but we fail to talk about the quality of life. How do we help people enhance the quality of life when they are at the crossroads of what has ended and what is yet to come? It is our responsibility as a Christian community, the church –

God's chosen means for changing the world, to take initiative on this endeavor.

Just as secret service personnel can teach us about having anticipatory vision, SPIES teach us about the aging process, too. What do SPIES do? They sometimes go undercover or on scouting trips to get information. As noted earlier, there is a necessity in gathering appropriate internal and external demographic data and hearing the voices of the Baby Boomers, as well as the existing population of older adults. That undercover scouting work is vital to developing a ministry that provides access points for many.

> THERE IS A NECESSITY IN GATHERING APPROPRIATE DEMOGRAPHIC INFORMATION AND HEARING THE VOICES OF THE BABY BOOMERS, AS WELL AS THE EXISTING POPULATION OF OLDER ADULTS.

The acrostic SPIES provides us with a framework for planning that can be used as we envision ministries for persons in their pre-retirement and retirement years.

S.PIES

S = SPIRITUAL

Spirituality is the core of our being. We need to become who God called us to be, heeding the Apostle Paul's words:

> *But one thing I do: Forgetting what is behind and straining toward what is ahead, I press on toward the goal to win the prize for which God has called me heavenward in Christ Jesus.*
>
> *(Philippians 3:13b-14 NIV)*

If we imagine a circle with God as the center, we do not want to stay on the circumference of the circle! We must move toward the center and ultimately live out of it. Our outward living is an overflow of God's work in us. God will be our home in *this life* in the midst of our anxious world. As Henri Nouwen suggests in *"Lifesigns"*:

Home is the place where we do not have to be afraid.
Home is the place where we can let our defenses down.
Home is the place where we can be free.
Home is the place where we can laugh and cry.
Home is where complete joy can be known.

We are not to be nomadic wanderers in this life; God wants us to be journeyers who are intentionally moving toward the center, our home with Him. Churches and

Christian organizations need to apply the same level of expertise they've used to discover generational differences (used to help nurture the spiritual growth of children and youth), to understanding the differences of older people. The local church can provide opportunities for learning from one another's faith stories – the stories of people sustaining faith through the ups and downs of life over thirty, forty, fifty, sixty, or more years.

Whatever approach we take in planning older adult ministry, there has to be a SPIRITUAL component. For those who follow Christ Jesus, regardless of age, there is a clear call to further His mission of making more disciples. Many have not been introduced to Jesus, or have not chosen to follow Him. This includes many within the circle of peers for both Baby Boomers and the Silent Generation (seventy and over). As we continue to help persons grow spiritually, we must be engaged in both intentional evangelism and discipleship.

Growth as a disciple will result in a deeper inward journey that leads us to an outward focus on others. In addition to helping others take one step closer to Christ, an outward focus includes service. As Richard Foster described the discipline of service in his book, *"Celebration of Discipline"*, it is clear that service, for a Christian, is not an option, it is a way of life. The options about service include only: where does one serve, who does one serve, and how much time is invested in service? Foster further notes that "the risen Christ beckons us to the ministry of the towel *(i.e., to SERVANTHOOD!)* It's a matter of obedience.

Another outward manifestation of the inner journey is reconciliation, not only with family and friends, but with those we do not know, many of whom are from different races, cultures, and socioeconomic classes. As Parker Palmer writes in *"Leading from Within"*:

> *"We share responsibility for creating the external world by projecting either a spirit of light or a spirit of shadow on that which is 'other' than us."*

An obedient disciple keeps growing and projects a spirit of light. Growth occurs in one's relationship to God, relationship with God's family, home or neighborhood life, and relationship to the world.

SP.IES

P=PHYSICAL

For older adults, regular physical activity is a key ingredient to maintaining one's health and well being. Physical activity can prevent many of the issues that may accompany the aging process. "Regular" is the operative word.

In the book, *"Outliers"*, author, Malcolm Gladwell, says that it takes roughly ten thousand hours of practice to achieve mastery in a field. That concept can be applied to physical exercise, as much as to other habits. Practice doesn't necessarily make perfect, but it does make a difference. Yes, as we age, physical activity does get harder, but there are adaptations such as exercises while sitting on a chair, including yoga. Taking a good thirty-minute walk, no matter what the speed, is helpful every day. Strength and stamina can be maintained and even increased.

Other important "to dos" which enhance physical well being include:

- Proper sleep
- Proper foods and the appropriate amounts of such *(Often, reeducation is needed to understand proper diet and nutrition at an older age)*
- Regular check-ups with doctors and a dentist

Directly related to physical well-being is an additional dimension that deserves attention: ***fall prevention***. Older persons need to view falls and the fear of falling as controllable. They should set realistic goals to increase activity, change their environments to reduce the risk factors associated with falling, and exercise to increase strength and balance.

Staying fit is a proven means for maintaining one's health and extending life. Even those who don't start regular physical practices until their 80s and 90s can alter their futures. The human body really is truly fearfully and wonderfully made.

SPI.ES

I=INTELLECTUAL

We have a mind—a brain capable of thought—and, contrary to what many believe, our brain cells keep growing. Intellectual wellness should be fostered in much the same way as one's physical wellness. Opportunities can be created to help people maintain engagement in creative and stimulating mental activities, expand their knowledge bases, and use multiple resources to learn more about the world around them. The growth mindset interventions developed by Carol Dweck of Stanford University are being applied primarily to adolescents and college students. Yet, she has noted that they could readily be adapted for working with mid-life and older adults to address issues of memory loss and cognitive decline. Again, this is a signal of the importance of replacing the *myths* about old age with *truths* in order to avoid fixed mindsets.

All persons, regardless of age, can continue to stimulate brain activity by engaging in activities that challenge and expand the thought processes. There are benefits beyond the entertainment of watching quiz shows like ***Jeopardy***. These types of shows provide opportunities for recall in answering questions. Other activities also valuable in intellectual stimulation include:

- Playing strategy board or computer games
- Doing crossroad puzzles
- Completing word searches

We can add to that list a variety of means for expanding knowledge through reading, watching documentaries, listening to TED talks, attending lectures, and even enrolling in college courses or continuing education offerings. *NetWellness*, associated with the University of Ohio, has reported that two decades of research indicates that *"healthy older brains are often as good as or better than younger brains in a wide variety of tasks."*

SPIE.S

E = EMOTIONAL

In his book, *"Childhood and Society,"* Erik Erikson discusses the balancing of extremes in each of life's stages. It is not that one side wins, but rather that the tension is maintained between the extremes.

- A small child wrestles between trust and mistrust
- For the adolescent, there is a struggle between identity and role confusion
- Middle-aged persons have tension between generativity and self-absorption

Middle-age is when preparation should begin for the next phase of life - old age. The way the extremes balance in this stage could adversely affect the tensions of old age. The tendency of many in middle age is to become self-absorbed, which leads to stagnation. It is often called a "cocooning" or "garage door" group. These are persons immersed in the workplace who can't wait to get home, close the door, and be alone. This isolation can lead to stagnation, or a feeling of being satisfied with the way things are. Generativity points, however, to getting out beyond ourselves, often through grandparenting, socializing with friends, or engaging in some form of volunteer work. For anyone who has experienced surgeries that require physical therapy, there is a keen awareness of how atrophy sets in if one is not engaged in regular therapy. So can it be with our life interests and passions.

The eighth stage, per Erikson's theory, is "old age," during which the task at hand is to balance the extremes of integrity and despair. Integrity implies acceptance of a life well-lived, acknowledging regrets, but not dwelling on them. Despair is a lack of future hope and a sense of not having lived a full and meaningful life. In despair, one gets buried in his or her regrets.

In Erikson's last book, "*The Life Cycle Completed*", his wife, Joan, added a "ninth stage" that applied to people who had become very old. She wrote:

> *"Old age in one's eighties and nineties brings with it new demands, reevaluations, and daily difficulties . . . in the ninth stage, the despair of stage eight is magnified by the experience of one's deteriorating body and mind, which results in a lowering of self-esteem and confidence. The wise course of action suggested for one's ninth stage, is*

> *to face down despair with faith and appropriate humility."*

We can add Paul Tournier's wisdom to these words:

> *"People are reluctant to talk about old age and death because they are afraid of emotion, and they willingly avoid things about which they feel the most emotional. These are the very things that most need discussion."*

The question for those of us working with older adults is, *"How can we nurture this healthy frame of mind among older adults and shape the expectations of those around them to avoid isolationism and feelings of worthlessness?"*

SPIES.

S = SOCIAL

The social part of one's life is critical to avoid growing lonely. Harvard Medical School professor and researcher, Robert Waldinger, recently reported[1] on results from a seventy-five year ongoing study of Harvard Medical School with 724 men. Eighty of the men are now in their nineties.

---

[1] *"What Makes a Good Life? Lessons from the Longest Study on Happiness" Robert Waldinger: Harvard University, Web. 2016.*

The major finding of the study was that the key to happiness is good relationships, regardless of socioeconomic status.

Relationships not only will keep us happier, but also healthier. Waldinger indicated that persons socially connected to family, to friends, and to community are happier, physically healthier, and they live longer than people who are less well connected. In the study, they also learned that the experience of loneliness turns out to be toxic. Waldinger noted that it is not necessarily being in committed relationships, but the quality of close relationships, that matters. Those for whom nurturing close relationships in their fifties was a priority, proved to be the happiest and healthiest in their eighties. Although the study focused on males, there is circumstantial evidence that the same findings hold true for females.

> CREATING COMMUNITY MUST BE AN INTENTIONAL UNDERTAKING IF ONE IS TO ENGAGE JOYFULLY ALL THE DAYS OF HIS OR HER LIFE.

Creating community must be an *intentional* undertaking if one is to engage joyfully all the days of his or her life. Planning for nurturing relationships is purposefully deciding to build a BRIDGE to connect to the world around you.

- **B**e welcoming to new people
- **R**eceive input and learn from new people
- **I**nitiate common interest groups in your circle of influence
- **D**evelop closer relationships with family and long-term friends
- **G**row closer in new relationships while grieving the losses of moves, illnesses, and death (create new beginnings)
- **E**xpand connections outside of your existing community to enlarge your sphere of care

The bottom-line? Be social. Our social network is our safety network.

QUESTIONS FOR REFLECTION

Think for yourself . . .

How are you personally pursuing growth in each of the SPIES dimensions?

SPIRITUAL?

PHYSICAL?

INTELLECTUAL?

EMOTIONAL?

SOCIAL?

Consider the bigger picture . . .

What current ministries address each of the SPIES dimensions?

SPIRITUAL?

PHYSICAL?

INTELLECTUAL?

EMOTIONAL?

SOCIAL?

Imagine how it could change . . .

What ministries by, with, and for older adults and pre-retirees need to be continued and strengthened? Started? Stopped?

CHAPTER 6

From Vision to Action

Do not go where the path may lead, go instead where there is no path and leave a trail.

~Ralph Waldo Emerson

Planning ministries to serve the evolving interests and needs of the "new old" (Baby Boomers who have been turning sixty-five since 2011) and those who are seventy plus, many of whom reject the ageist stereotypes, is uncharted territory. It is critical in the planning process to have a guide and a map with signposts noting "places to visit" along the way. The guide is a leadership team of persons who are passionate about helping persons experience vital living all the days of their lives.

CREATING AND EQUIPPING THE TEAM

Experience has shown that a well-developed ministry leadership team is necessary for an older adult ministry to get traction and flourish. In situations where a strong team is not in place, the ministry is likely to sputter and not flourish.

A team should include five to nine persons representing a broad age spectrum from fifty to age eighty-five and over. Primary characteristics to be sought in the team members, in addition to passion and sense of call to this area of ministry, include:

- A personal modeling of purposeful living
- Capacity to create a mental picture of a desired future
- Organizational skills to develop implementation plans
- The ability to inspire others to act

Once a team is recruited, it is critical to engage in the team-building process as well as equip them for the task. Team building includes experiences that help the members grow in understanding: a) their purpose, b) the context of those they will serve, c) other members within the team, and d) themselves. Even after an initial intensive focus on team building, it is highly recommended that each meeting of the team include a short time focused on team building.

The initial equipping of a team can best be accomplished through a three- to four-hour learning experience that includes explorations of a number of topics relevant to the older adult ministries. A basic session outline could include the following:

- Biblical insights for later years of life
- History of retirement as an "official" part of life
- Myths and realities of aging today
- Demographic trends both inside and outside the church's community
- Framework for a wholistic ministry by, with, and for older adults
- Starter ministry ideas

A summary of forming a leadership team for this ministry is given in Appendix A at the back of the book. Additional information on teams and team building is available on the Electronic Resource Hub referenced at the beginning of the book.

GATHERING BACKGROUND INFORMATION

The next step in the team's planning process is two-fold. First, it is necessary to gather specific demographic information for the individual church context, as well as for the community served by the church. Second, it's important to solicit the thoughts and feelings among those within the existing Baby Boomer and sixty-five and over constituency via focus groups and surveys. The themes within the results of this data gathered, by either the entire team or subgroups within the team, can provide a backdrop to engage in the visioning process for the future. A sample worksheet, *Looking at Your Church*, to summarize data is available on the Electronic Resource Hub.

VISION TO ACTION

Signposts noting "places to visit" along the journey are vital to staying on track. The first signpost is at the beginning of the journey – prayer. It is God's direction that you are discerning for a particular place with a particular people at a particular time.

> *Ask and it will be given to you; seek and you will find; knock and the door will be opened to you.*
> *(Matthew 7:7 NIV)*

Prayer continues as you visit the other places along the way and throughout the implementation. After initiating prayer, there are 4 Ps as suggested by William Bridges in the preparing for a new beginning.

Prayer: What are the specific areas for prayer focus? As a team? As a church? As an individual?

Purpose: Why are we doing this? What are we trying to accomplish?

Picture: What is the end result? How is it going to work?

Plan: What is the detailed road map for getting to where we need to go? What is going to happen over the next few months? What happens first, second, third?

Part: What is my role? How will I be involved? What are the roles of others?

PURPOSE

The recruitment process for the team should have included a statement of general purpose. The initial team building process needs to include a discussion of the question, *Why do we exist?* Even with this initial groundwork, though, it is wise to allow the team to engage in a process of clarifying or refining their own purpose statement (often referred to as a mission) before proceeding with the rest of the planning process.

Given the data gathered, both quantitative and qualitative, the specific details of a team's purpose (or mission) may need to be revised. One approach is to present the team with the draft purpose statement and engage the group in giving feedback to ultimately add, delete, and refine the statement until a point of consensus for moving forward with the stated purpose (mission).

CREATING A PICTURE

As has already been shared, a vision is a mental picture of a preferred future. That preferred future must be based on anticipatory vision, not solely on what is past or present. One of the most helpful ways to engage a team in visioning is to have individuals commit five to seven minutes to reflecting on and responding on a pictured future that takes into consideration what one can imagine sensing.

Consider a simple journal prompt as follows:

> *In the year (choose date at least five years in the future), in relation to ministries to, with, and by the sixty-five and older congregation, and*

preparation of Baby Boomers for this next phase,

I See...
I Feel...
I Hear...

After individuals have completed writing their vision statements, invite each to read the vision to other team members, with encouragement that other team members listen for themes in what emerges from all. After reading the visions, identify common themes.

An alternative approach to the visioning process is to have each person write his or her vision statement on a sheet of paper silently for several minutes. Each person then passes his or her paper on to a neighbor. The neighbor underlines the key words and phrases they like best. Pass the statements on to the next person, who will also underline key words and phrases. Repeat until everyone has seen (and underlined) everyone else's vision statement. Use a clarifying and combining exercise to get the common phrases and words identified and begin crafting a single vision statement together.

To translate the common themes of a vision statement to the team's desired outcomes, engage team members in writing specific, measurable, and observable desired outcomes, or goals related to each theme.

DEVELOPING A PLAN

The next step for the leadership team is generating possibilities, in order to enable the process of moving toward the desired outcomes. As with finalizing a purpose and vision, there are multiple ways to generate possibilities.

After generating a listing of possibilities, have the group engage in a prioritizing exercise to discern which idea(s) to explore first. This exercise is completed with the gentle reminder that we can do anything, but we can't do everything. A variety of approaches to generating possibilities and prioritizing are provided in Appendix B. Once the top three to five priority action items have been identified, the team can proceed toward developing specific action plans noting what will happen by when and who is responsible.

At this point, it may become necessary to divide a team into subgroups with specific assignments for detailing the plans. It is normal and natural for some to have greater interest and expertise in specific areas. A sample Action Plan worksheet is available on the Electronic Resource Hub.

IMPLEMENTING THE PLAN

A strategy for implementation is often the missing element of a planning process. The excitement that is generated during the visioning exercise and exploring possibilities can wane during the detailing of an action plan. Yet, without implementation, the vision can't happen.

- *Starting up a new initiative amid rapid change has challenges; "Go slow to go fast," is a wise mantra used by many*
- *Start small with your ministry and let the word spread; identify one initiative to pilot. This singular effort will help to give focus to content, audience, and needed buy-in from legitimizers (persons whose endorsement can make a difference in the big picture)*
- *Engage in an ongoing review and thorough evaluation at its completion to discern needed adjustments or, if necessary, stops*
- *Successes provide stories to validate the new initiative and enable the circle of legitimizers to increase; success stories become the rich soil in which other new initiatives can be planted*
- *Learnings from failure can also be significant. Failures should serve as a shared learning that can be the catalyst for revision of plans and the most effective future launches*

We live in a rapidly changing environment which requires ongoing revision and adaptation of our plans made today. As Jason Silva, a young television personality and filmmaker stated, "There's always going to be the circumstances you can't plan for. There's always the unexpected relevance and the serendipity." For those of us leading in the Christian community, serendipities are acknowledged as gifts from God.

QUESTIONS FOR REFLECTION

Think for yourself . . .

What are the assets you could bring to a leadership team for this ministry?

Consider the bigger picture . . .

Who are the persons that you believe are ready to assist with launching a new or revamped ministry with older adults? Preparing Baby Boomers for this next phase of life?

Imagine how it could change . . .

What challenges might come your way and how might you meet them?

CHAPTER 7

Ideas for a SPIES Ministry

We don't drift in good directions. We discipline and prioritize ourselves there.
~Andy Stanley

There are multiple possibilities for engagement of older adults to live into their purposes all the days of their lives. You can't do everything, so focus becomes important in determining how to best use a team's resources of time and energy. Ask yourselves which of the five areas of SPIES needs strengthening? What single item could be introduced that would meet a need and overcome the lacking area?

ULTIMATELY, THE IDEAL GOAL FOR A SPIES MINISTRY IS TO OFFER SOME FORM OF EXPERIENCE IN EACH OF THE FIVE AREAS...

Ultimately, the ideal goal for a SPIES ministry is to offer some form of experience in each of the five areas: spiritual, physical, intellectual, emotional, and social, while maintaining an overall balance.

SPIRITUAL

- Lifelong Learning Institutes (exploring areas like church history, themes in Bible, worship music, etc.)
    - Put on the hat of academic dean and create a nonacademic institute, perhaps nine months with three months off; develop courses and group studies that provide the stimuli for going deeper in understanding the Bible and the Christian Church, as well as addressing current societal issues from a Biblical perspective
- Discipleship Circles—
    - Using the small group format, invite five to seven persons to join in a *Discipleship Circle* for six weeks with six topics related to the Christian life in older adult years
- Spiritual practices—
    - Encourage older adults in prayer, meditation, study, fasting, journaling, and celebration; sponsor one-day seminars to introduce and review common spiritual practices
    - Offer opportunities for spiritual direction
- Outward Focus—
    - Offer older adults opportunities to explore their gifts and passions allowing them to discern areas for serving; arrange possibilities for testing out gift sets in

service before making either short-term or long-term commitments

- Create multiple short-term service opportunities to accommodate the varying schedules of older adults
- Provide educational opportunities to increase awareness of other races and cultures with partners from such races and cultures for debriefing
- Invite persons to make presentations on local justice issues with guidance for how to get involved
- Provide equipping sessions for sharing one's faith
- Create opportunities for persons to invite those who are not believers to experience relationships with believers
- Look for service activities in the community where people can be involved in a collaborative way

PHYSICAL

- Exercise classes—
  - Tap into the benefits of having a multipurpose room or similar-sized room to offer classes in weight lifting, basic exercise, chair yoga, Pilates, and Tai Chi

- Proper eating habits—
  - Offer lectures from dieticians or other persons knowledgeable about nutrition
  - Invite a local chef or someone within your own congregation to provide cooking classes to equip persons for cooking nutritional food
- Walking partners—
  - Create opportunities for persons to partner with others to engage in walking inside or outside the church; offer refreshments and fellowship after the scheduled walks
- Availability of treadmills—
  - If you have extra space in your church facility, create an actual fitness center-with treadmills and other basic equipment; the relationships developed are an added SOCIAL byproduct
- Fall prevention—
  - Offer education regarding fall prevention, either as a program for a social event or at a separate time
- Home assessments to discern adaptability—
  - Invite an architect who is knowledgeable about creating handicapped accessible spaces to make a presentation and offer counsel to older adults desiring to age in place

- Home care services—
  - Create a network of older adults who are mobile and able physically to serve as nonmedical caregivers; this service could be similar to *Stephen Ministry*, but enhanced through adding transportation to doctors, grocery stories, and necessity shopping
- Wellness checkups for blood pressure, weight, and other vital statistics—
  - Arrange with local medical centers for providing basic "wellness checkups" at your church
- End of life decisions—
  - Invite both medical personnel and legal advisors to provide a session or sessions to help persons learn about and actually complete advance directives

INTELLECTUAL

- Book Clubs—
  - Identify general interests of older adult readers and initiate short-term book clubs where persons come together to reflect on a particular book they are reading in common
- Continuing Education Offerings—
  - As noted within the spiritual dimension, be your own academic dean and create nonacademic offerings on a regular basis to stimulate greater understanding of oneself,

others, and the world; choose topics that could be appealing to both believers and nonbelievers

- Teach Your Grandparents Day—
    - Younger generations can provide tech training and tech updates to the older adults in your community
    - Enlist your church's older children and teens to provide leadership for sessions to assist older adults with maximizing the use of their smart phones and computers for social networking, shopping, doing research, online bill payments and banking, maintaining records, etc.
    - Consider making the learning multi-generational and have the older adults bring a learning for the older children and teens
- Classes and seminars to develop new skills for part-time work or "encore careers"—
    - Identify the types of part-time positions open to older adults in your community and do research to identify the new skills that will be needed; provide training sessions focused on those new skills

- Film Clubs—
    - Identify the visual learners among your older adults, explore their interests, and create opportunities for groups to gather to watch and discuss films such as documentaries and recent films such as *"Creed"* and *"The Intern"*
- Travel with Lectures—
    - Identify the explorers among your older adults, identify geographic regions in which there is interest, and match a local expert with a learning tour
- Formal Classes—
    - Identify and publicize free tuition classes through local colleges, universities and specialty schools such as: culinary arts, auto repair, nursing, woodworking, writing and performance arts, and other continuing education offerings; provide transportation and study times for your older adults

EMOTIONAL

- Offer support groups and classes focusing on:
    - Caregiving
    - Learning to Grieve
    - Being Single Again (widowed or divorced)
    - Being A Family Again (remarriage)
    - Managing Transitions
    - Re-creating Purpose and Sense of Self

  - Having Difficult Conversations
  - Death and Dying
  - Growing a Marriage in the Latter Phase of Life
  - Relating to Children and Grandchildren
  - Parenting Grandchildren
- Offer pastoral counseling by persons skilled in working with older adults
- Provide spiritual directors

Social

- Create short-term (six to eight week) support groups or a series of classes or one-day seminars focused on:
  - Recreating Community (when your family and friends die before you)
  - Geographic Community (establishing oneself in relocation)
  - Topical Community (housing decisions, medical issues, being a caregiver, and financial planning)
  - Stage Community (subgroupings by age within older adults)
  - Professional Community (profession and industry-specific common connections)
  - Cultivating NEW Relationships Without Fear
  - Cross-Cultural Relationships

    - Intergenerational Relationships
- Celebrate holidays throughout the year with social gatherings for older adults
- Have an intergenerational experience with children or youth at a Valentine's Party or a Grandparent-Grandchild party with a unique theme
- Create occasional game nights with prizes to add to the fun
- Plan outings for lovers of sports, the theater, museums, music, food festivals, and other social events

The possibilities are endless. Choose a few that will provide access points for those you are serving and that fit the local culture.

ASSISTING THE YOUNGER AND MIDDLE BOOMERS

Although a number of the starter ideas listed for a SPIES ministry could be adapted to fit a younger and middle Baby Boomer age group below age sixty-five, several key areas need to be added to address the new young old.

Some of these additions include:

- Raising awareness about the need for future planning in areas such as having conversations about wishes if incapacitated or upon death with parents, children, or trusted friends, financial planning, and adapting housing to age in place;

Appendices C, D, and E provide further information about these topics

- Addressing the myths that create barriers in the growing old process
- Thinking and praying about identity
- Considering God's lifelong calling

There is a future to be created. As John F. Kennedy said, "change is the law of life. And those who look only to the past or present are certain to miss the future."

The law of change is real not only for individuals, but also for churches and other organizations.

QUESTIONS FOR REFLECTION

Think for yourself . . .

Which 2-3 ideas listed would create a meaningful connection for you at this point in your journey?

Consider the bigger picture...

Which dimension(s) of SPIES do you sense need to be enhanced first in your ministry with the sixty-five and older population? And for the trailing edge and middle Baby Boomers?

Imagine how it could change...

If you did not have any existing ministries for the sixty-five and older population, or middle age, how would you start to create a wholistic approach using the SPIES framework?

PART III
Existing and Emerging Ministries

Don't be a prisoner of the past, become a pioneer of the future.

~Farshad Asl

CHAPTER 8

Existing Ministries

Real fellowship is more than attending services or having a potluck together. It is experiencing life together.

~PLUS@PCC

The stories that follow are based on the information provided by the founding leaders of two, strong, existing ministries for older adults.

PLUS@PCC[1]
A Ministry of Peninsula Covenant Church
Redwood City, California

In early spring 2004, the senior pastor, Gary Gaddini, of Peninsula Covenant Church approached Rod Toews, a staff person at the church, with the request, "Would you begin an older adult ministry?" At the time, more than fifty percent of the congregation of almost 1000 worship attendees was over fifty years of age.

The first step taken by Rod was to contact an outside consultant, Alan Forsman. Twenty adults, age fifty and over, were invited to gather and talk about a potential ministry.

---

[1] *Information provided by Rod Toews, founding leader of PLUS*

The consultant was invited to the next organizational meeting and a subsequent meeting with twelve selected potential leaders.

Shortly after the initial discussions, Alan and the twelve leaders met to formulate a plan for ministry. The name, PLUS, was chosen with a mission articulated as follows:

> *"A community of those over fifty in which God's purposes for their lives are fulfilled through fellowship, spiritual growth, service and fun."*

September 2004 was set as the PLUS launch date.

From the church directory, a potential list of participants was selected and they were invited to a free launch luncheon of PLUS with the explanation of "we want to add a PLUS to their lives."

Again, the consultant was present and spoke at the luncheon. The potential ministry was outlined and the leaders were introduced. One couple had given $5000 seed money for the luncheon. The original database included more than 300 people. Overall, people were enthusiastic and affirmed the ministry. Likewise, the people were responsive to ideas and the leaders. The consultant, along with the leaders, provided expertise needed for implementing an older adult ministry.

During the course of ten years after its beginnings, PLUS was developed to address the felt needs of the persons involved. Activities included Sunday school classes by age, concerts, fellowship, and fun activities, discipleship, outreach, mission trips, and international tours. One of the key desired outcomes was achieved – people in the fifty plus age group were made to feel significant! The ministry is now being led by a new pastor. New vision with new ideas has shaped new programming. Yet, the mission remains the same.

PEOPLE IN THE FIFTY PLUS AGE GROUP WERE MADE TO FEEL SIGNIFICANT!

PLUS@PCC continues to be a community of those over fifty in which God's purposes for their lives are fulfilled through fellowship, spiritual growth, service, and fun. Their vision is to encourage people fifty and above to discover and actively pursue God's purposes for their lives.

The description of PLUS@PCC given on the church's website describes the underlying conviction. "One of the main purposes in the life of a church community is to expand opportunities for full participation in the fellowship of that body. Real fellowship is more than attending services or having a potluck together. It is experiencing life together."

TREK[1]
Harbor Covenant Church
Gig Harbor, Washington

The seeds for TREK, a ministry for those fifty plus, were planted at a staff retreat when the group identified and discussed a growing nationwide population emerging with 10,000 people turning sixty-five years of age each day in our country. Considering this fact and the significant number of older adults already attending Harbor Covenant Church, the Senior Pastor and Sammi McCubbins, the Director of Pastoral Care, began to discuss the need for an older adult ministry that would connect older adults attending Harbor Covenant and reach out to older adults in the community.

Sammi began to pray about whom to ask to serve on such a team and how such a ministry would incorporate the church's organizing principles: *reach people for Christ, make disciples and live a lifestyle of compassion, mercy, and justice.*

First, older adults who were thinking about retiring or who had recently retired were invited to a *Success to Significance* luncheon that focused on how older adults today were moving beyond the first half, in the game of life, into a time of revitalization. People who attended this luncheon and who were interested in this more vibrant older adult lifestyle were invited to join this upcoming older adult ministry leadership team along with other hand-picked team members.

---

[1] *Information provided by Sammi McCubbins, Director of Pastoral Care*

The leadership team met for eighteen months before the launching of the older adult ministry named TREK with a purpose of being a group of people who enjoy being together having fun while growing in their faith and reaching out to people in the community. The purpose statement incorporates the organizing principles of the church. It was launched during fall kick-off with a special celebration and a calendar of events that invited people to join in the TREK activities. Dimensions that have emerged include:

- Building fellowship among people both inside and outside the church which encourages inviting friends and neighbors to the TREK excursions
- Providing relevant enrichment opportunities appropriate for older adult living through forums, speakers and classes (spiritual, financial, family)
- Creating recreational outings that attract older adults and build community
- Involving older adults in service projects in the community

The signs of effectiveness with TREK have included:

- The growing level of enthusiasm expressed by the leadership team since launching the ministry
- Growing efforts to invite friends from outside the church to TREK events
- "Let's do this again" (positive feedback from attendees)

- "We need more tables" (higher than expected turnout to events)

The future hope for TREK is continued effectiveness in current dimensions with expansion into service, outreach, and collaborative efforts. There is anticipation of the TREK service component to continue growing, as the church begins a pre-school program and identifies ways volunteers can help. The outreach component is expected to grow now that people know more about TREK and what it offers to older adults. TREK will be collaborating with the new older adult housing project coming into the community in the fall and the co-sponsoring of an *Older Adult Safety Internet Conference*. The potential for other such gatherings in the future is promising.

The name, TREK, signals moving forward and that is the nature of the individuals participating, as well as the team providing leadership. As the church's website description of TREK ends:

Life is an adventure ... Join us!

CHAPTER 9

Emerging Ministries

There needed to be something that met the spiritual needs of older adults, not just in the church, but for the local community as well.

~Renee Roeschley

The stories that follow are based on information provided by the current leaders of emerging ministries in the area of older adult ministry.

JOURNEYS For Adults 50+[1]
Salem Covenant Church
New Brighton, Minnesota

The seeds for JOURNEYS were planted during the church's strategic planning process initiated by the Leadership Team to discern what areas of focus would help their church increase effectiveness in fulfilling its mission. The result from a look at the external community was that one of the largest and fastest growing populations in the church's community

---

[1] *Information provided by Jonna Fantz, staff, and Sue Poston, team leader for JOURNEYS*

was people headed into retirement. This also was one of the largest percentages within the existing congregation.

Internally, the current Senior Fellowship Team, while implementing great monthly Friday lunch events, were noticing declining numbers and an increasing average age of the older adults that attended. The Senior Fellowship ministry team stated they knew that something needed to be done for older adults who didn't have mobility issues, but that was just not what their team was called to do.

At the end of the strategic planning process, the outreach and community life pastor, Jonna Fantz was charged with "getting the ball rolling" to form a new ministry team. After conversations with Jonna and the senior pastor, Mark Pattie, Sue Poston, an active retiree engaged in a vital life of her own, committed to serve as leader of this new team.

Sue was motivated by the challenge to chart a new way to do ministry to people in the third phase of their adult lives. Sue also felt like she had not connected well with her own peer group in this age. She sensed this was an invitation from God to connect more deeply, herself, while helping others to do the same.

Forming a Leadership Team specifically for this new ministry was a priority. Sue and Jonna brainstormed a listing of potential team members. They added to that list other people whose voices needed to be heard. An invitation was sent for a focus group and dessert night. Twelve people attended that session.

Sue guided the conversation and Jonna recorded on newsprint ideas that surrounded four questions:

- What is it that you are currently involved in that brings meaning and joy to your life?
- What are you hungry to know more about?
- What issues are you confronting?
- What is missing for your age group in Salem's ministries in these three areas:
    - SPIRITUAL FORMATION
    - FUN AND FELLOWSHIP
    - SERVICE
- Share general comments, hopes, dreams, fears, etc.

The evening stimulated great conversation with honest and open sharing. Sue followed up by pursuing people who attended that evening to be on the team, and others that couldn't attend the focus group, but were interested. A team of ten persons joined Sue for the adventure of building this new ministry.

Salem Covenant then extended an invitation to Evelyn Johnson and Alan Forsman to lead a retreat to launch this new leadership team. They were to provide some education to help this team learn more about this demographic and to inspire them toward a vision of what was possible in this ministry. They also were tasked with helping the team to build community and begin the ministry planning process.

The team met on a Saturday in late February for six hours. It was a powerful time of launching and bonding. There was lots of great learning and key issues emerged, such as how to name the ministry. The team engaged in great discussion about the older adult demographic and what aging myths existed in Salem Covenant Church. The team agreed to meet again following Easter.

The first regular team meeting ended up focusing on what kind of event should be done as an interest raising event. *JOURNEYS For Adults 50+* emerged as the name of the ministry with a stated purpose:

> *JOURNEYS exists to provide connecting opportunities through a wholistic ministry within and beyond the Salem community to strengthen spiritual growth, stimulate intellectual curiosity, promote healthy living, and enrich social, community and missional involvement.*

As meetings progressed, the team decided to do a survey on Sunday morning and offer cinnamon rolls as a hospitality and gathering piece.

To date, the key outcome from JOURNEYS For Adults 50+ has been a team which has bonded and is full of good ideas.

The future is embedded in the phrase, *"coming soon."*

With Age...[1]
A Collaborative Ministry
Chicago, Illinois

Senior Share, a formation group for older adults at Grace Covenant Church in Chicago, was started in 2003 by Renee Roeschley. In the beginning, the make-up of the group was primarily people from the church. However, as the years passed, its composition evolved and now most members of the group are from the local community. During the process of leading this group, Renee noted the importance of older adults having a place to meet spiritual needs through sharing and reflecting on God's presence in their life stories with peers.

She also began to notice that there were a limited number of ministries available, and even those that had started in the local church for older adults were not sustained. Another observation was the absence of a "place" for older adults at many levels in the church, much like what it looks like in our society.

Renee became burdened with a sense that there could be so much more than what is offered for older adults, in the church, by the government agencies, and through nonprofits. There needed to be something that met the spiritual needs of older adults, not just in the church, but for the local community as well. She believed the church was the perfect vessel to do this.

---

[1] *Information provided by Renee Roeschley and Mary Jane Dawson, Leaders*

Renee always felt that she could not start something like this alone. No one "caught the vision," until she shared it with Mary Jane Dawson who co-facilitates the Senior Share group at Grace.

They did not follow up on this desire until summer of 2015, when—in a coaching session with Troy Cady of the nonprofit, "Playfull"—Renee talked about it. Troy sensed her passion and the vision that God had entrusted to her. Troy encouraged her to think of others that could join her in collaborating. She invited Mary Jane for more conversation and, together, they began to plan a time when others would be invited to a series of listening groups to discuss the needs of older adults.

During coaching sessions with Troy, Renee and Mary Jane made a list of people to invite to be part of a group to explore the needs of older adults in Chicago. Many accepted their invitation and the first meeting was in October of 2015.

In the group there are and have been social workers, pastors, people who work directly with older adults in a facility environment, and several older adults of various backgrounds such as teaching, administration and banking.

In the time since Troy finished coaching the two women and leading the listening group exploration, Renee and Mary Jane have taken turns leading parts of each meeting and are inviting other members who are willing to lead certain topics.

One of the first steps was discerning a mission statement for the group with all team members contributing in the creating of a draft, revising, and ultimately affirming a final mission. At the same time, the group generated a listing of potential names for the ministry and—by consensus—affirmed the chosen name. Thus, the birth of the new collaborative ministry with a name and a mission:

WITH AGE...

> *"Our mission is to create a space where older adults explore and affirm their identity and purpose, find voice and grow spiritually as engaged members of their communities."*

During the process, some of the noteworthy dimensions of ministry that are emerging include:

- Serving populations: newly retired and older
- Programs or ministries started by *With Age...*, and potentially with the church, for the local community on the north side of Chicago
- Projects that focus on exploring purpose and identity at "this time in life"

In a reasonable projected amount of time, the group plans to use one or two of the proposed programs that were identified in the process of the listening groups facilitated by Troy Cady. At the present time, Renee and Mary Jane are assessing the strengths of the core group to determine what skills and strengths exist in setting up the programs, advertising them, and other details necessary to carry them out.

Before the programs are started, attendance goals will be set. In addition, evaluations will be requested from those who attend to adequately monitor, 1) staying true to the mission of *With Age...*, and 2) to aid the implementation team in making needed changes and to determine if the programs are making a difference.

To date, the key outcomes have been:

- a solid and dedicated core group of six to seven individuals that work well together
- a name, mission statement, and twice monthly meetings
- several proposed programs that align with the mission statement

In summary, creating *With Age...* has been a process of observing older adults, discerning personal passions, receiving coaching, listening to the voices of others, sharing ideas, and deciding together!

All of these steps have shaped the hope to fully develop programming by the end of 2016 for implementation in early 2017.

AN INSIDE LOOK AT AGING [1]
For Middle Adults
A Plan for Helping with the Task of Caregiving

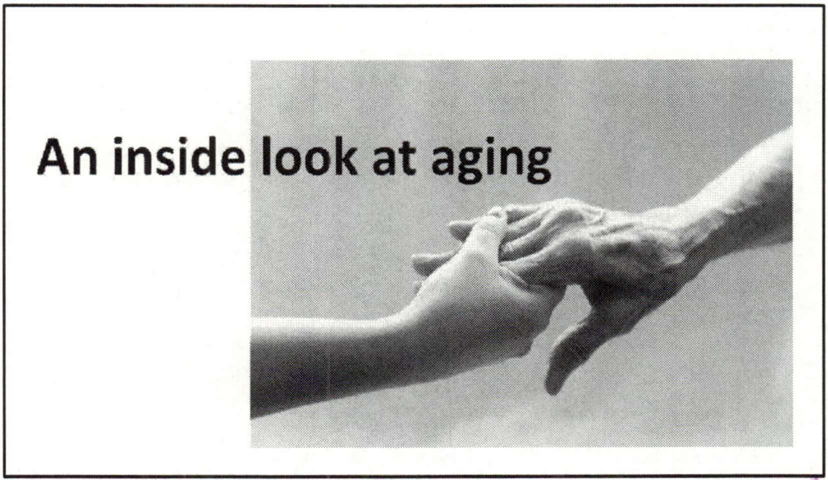

We live in a youth-obsessed culture. But what does life look like for those who are in the later phase of aging? This is a key question if we are to engage with, serve and learn from those who are older adults.

For those of us with aging parents, as well as those of us who are looking ahead to the later seasons of life, getting some perspective on aging can be a source of help, comfort and motivation.

The two one-hour sessions were designed to focus on the challenges and opportunities of aging in today's society and solutions and perspectives.

---

[1] *Information was provided by Steve Wong, designer and teacher of the sessions.*

The first session explored a wide range of topics including:

- Thinking about aging using a TED talk, *"What really matters at the end of life"*
- Describing aging using the author Atul Gawande's book, "*Being Mortal*", Erik Erikson's eight stages, and reflections on 1 John 2:12-14
- A case study in aging focused on Felix Silverstone, from Atul Gawande's book
- The local church and those who are aging with reflections on the SPIES framework given in this book

The second session focused on external solutions and internal perspectives. Resources used included:

- *"Brief but Spectacular"* video by Flossie Lewis[1]
- Dr. Bill Thomas's story
- General information about assisted living from "*Being Mortal*"
- Excerpts from Joan Chittister's book, "*The Gift of Years*"
- Joan Erikson's summary of a ninth stage addition, gerotranscendence, to her husband, Erik's, original eight stages.

Find the above list of resources on the EVAL Ministries Electronic Resource Hub.

[1] *Flossie Lewis' story is one of the "Brief but Spectacular" series of videos shown on the "PBS Newshour" at* http://www.pbs.org/newshour/brief/page/3 *or on YouTube:* https://www.youtube.com/watch?v=oeUc7hjYLbI.

At the close of the second session, the question to be asked is "What are up to three things that I will do in the next couple of weeks as a result of these sessions and why?"

Since the initial preparation of the sessions, Pastor Wong has expanded the series to three sessions with addition of more information regarding the ninth stage.

~~~~

There is much on the horizon to celebrate, anticipate, and create. ***Let's wake up, join these pioneers, and go confidently into the future!***
~~~~

PART IV
Resources and Reflecting

"To God be the glory, great things He hath done."

~ Hymn by Frances Jane "Fanny" Crosby

ABOUT THE APPENDICES

What follows in the next several pages are some helpful tools for planning and implementing your own church's older adult ministries. Each of these tools are also accessible (and downloadable) on the Electronic Resource Hub (found by scanning the code at the right or by visiting: http://www.rejilaberje.com/eval-ministries.html or by scanning the below codes to the specific resources.

Appendix A – Building your older adult ministry team: http://nebula.wsimg.com/c8d82026b5631713365e7dbc86e6e7e6?AccessKeyId=45F3FFA35D60D3429469&disposition=0&alloworigin=1.

Appendix B – Brainstorming and prioritizing found at: http://nebula.wsimg.com/14e6cdf663b5299fc6cd63719faf5999?AccessKeyId=45F3FFA35D60D3429469&disposition=0&alloworigin=1

Appendix C – End of life decisions and discussions found at: http://nebula.wsimg.com/962e17ab92cdb2ada2ef9b565c3c95ce?AccessKeyId=45F3FFA35D60D3429469&disposition=0&alloworigin=1.

Appendix D – Assessing Finances and Preparing A Plan found at: http://nebula.wsimg.com/a8ea6b7fd1392996d584d58a2f3829da?AccessKeyId=45F3FFA35D60D3429469&disposition=0&alloworigin=1.

Appendix E – Adapting Housing for Accessibility found at: http://nebula.wsimg.com/6a6cb80044cfd66a03640f7db95f6de2?AccessKeyId=45F3FFA35D60D3429469&disposition=0&alloworigin=1.

APPENDIX A

Older Adult Ministry Team

Purpose: to gain input that will assist congregational leadership in discerning God's spiritual, strategic direction for the future of ministry by, with and for older adults

People: usually comprised of 5-9. The team is appointed (preferred). One member from leadership team or staff should be present as a liaison. The Older Adult Ministry Team is appointed by the church leadership team (LT) and is a recommending body whose findings will serve as input to the LT in their discernment of future direction.

Process: the team engages in assessing the internal environment of the congregation and external environments represented by the unique regions of the members and attendees. The focus is on determining the appropriate demographics.

Attention is given to learning from our history in order to inform our future. Throughout the process, "transparent" communication is essential. An intentional prayer effort should undergird all the work. The benefits are many. Fresh information is gathered. Current assumptions are verified or contradicted. Action indicates that there is a future and "we are moving ahead."

General tasks of the process are:

- Gathering fresh information--taking a new look at the current reality
- Maintenance--evaluating current ministries
- Enhancement --focus on a significant area (areas) which can engender future hope
- Readiness-- assessing history, identity, leadership, outside resources, new direction, openness to change

Related tasks include:

- Reducing Anxiety
- Assessing Infrastructures
- Attending to matters of Whole-Life Stewardship (which includes spiritual growth, service and giving)
- Enhancing Leadership Skills
- Focusing on Spiritual Needs (Prayer, Discipleship, Healing)

Participants:

- Positive influencers
- Intergenerational representation-from 50s-70s is recommended
- Diversity in gender, ethnicity, and time in the church (fresh eyes and ears encouraged)

Process:

- An initial orientation session to communicate the process and begin the work
- A monthly meeting to receive updates on progress
- Engaging a wider range of people in gathering information
- Working in subgroups according to interest and expertise
- Collating information and begin interpretation of the results-what patterns are emerging
- Send findings and recommendations to the LT
- Get buy in from LT and implement

APPENDIX B

Brainstorming and Prioritizing

Brainstorming

Nonjudgmental brainstorming is an effective way to gain input from a team. There are several effective processes.

Round Robin Approach

- The round robin approach works best with up to fifteen people. For more than that, additional groups could be created.
- Frame the question (i.e. "What type of activity would interest you?" or "What type of experience would meet your felt needs?")
- Craft a question for each of the areas in SPIES.
- Give people a couple of minutes to think. Ask for a volunteer to start. Stress that only one idea is shared initially. After the first person volunteers, set a pattern and go around the group until all ideas are stated.

Someone should facilitate the process and another should record the ideas on a flip chart or white board. Guidelines for brainstorming should be:

1. All ideas are honored and recorded
2. No debating of ideas as they are stated

After all ideas are recorded, there can be a process of clarifying and combining in preparation for a focusing activity.

AFFINITY DIAGRAM

Affinity diagrams are an alternative method of brainstorming.

- Frame the question as for brainstorming.
- Each person is given two large post-it notes that. After having a couple of minutes to think, they are to write one idea on each post-it. Ideas should be brief and should start with an actionable verb, i.e. improve communication, conduct focus groups, know our neighborhood.
- Collect the post-it notes, searching for group similarities and themes.
- Create categories from the clustered post-it notes.
- Discuss ideas for clarification.

FOCUSING

Whatever information gathering processes are used, it is essential to prioritize. A proven method to narrow an idea is "Divide by 3."

- Tabulate the total number of consolidated ideas. Divide by 3. If there are twenty-four ideas the number would be eight. Each person gets eight dots. There is one dot per vote. Walk around and place dots on the ideas (on post-its or flip charts). All dots should go on different ideas.
- There tends to be a cluster of three to five top ideas. From there, a next step would be a simple rank order. People can vote again, either with dots or with raising of hands to determine a consensus on top ideas.
- The votes should result in three areas for exploration.

APPENDIX C

End of Life Decisions and Having Conversations

"Later..."
"When the need arises..."
"All's well..."
"Not yet..."
"I'm too busy living..."

One or more of these responses may be what you've heard a spouse, parent, child, or friend say. Perhaps even you have said it. Unfortunately, those comments, and others like them, are common for a large segment of our population, when it comes to the area of communicating with family members and trusted friends about one's wishes, should he or she become incapacitated or die. In a recent Harris Survey completed for the National Endowment of Financial Services in March 2016, only 33% of the population of all ages have engaged in a conversation about this inevitable stage of life. The time is NOW, not later.

One of the first considerations for such a conversation is determining a Power of Attorney (POA). POA should be secured with legal advice, as opposed to simply completing a form found online. Different states have varying standards for types of Powers of Attorney and what they are allowed or not allowed to do.

Besides POAs for financial and legal matters, one should identify a medical or health care power of attorney. Medical or health care POAs are those trusted people named to make decisions for you when you are unable to do so.

Regardless of the type of POA, the missing link is often communication between spouses, parent and child, or trusted friends. Communication is needed for clarity and release from anxiety on the part of both.

In addition, one needs to maintain a clear, comprehensive list of assets, liabilities, account numbers, online account sign-in information (including usernames, passwords, and associated emails), insurance policies, and location of wills and trusts. Review the list with the chosen responsible person(s) who will be faced with a multitude of financial transactions and decisions upon your being incapacitated or dying.

Lastly, writing out your wishes for burial and discussing those wishes with one's spouse, children, or a trusted representative is another critical task on the "to do list." This becomes an extension of your care for them beyond your death. The immediate hours after one's death are filled with an overwhelming checklist for those responsible for burial. Providing this overview can alleviate anxiety and allow close family and friends to engage in the necessary work of mourning.

Having a conversation about being incapacitated or one's post-death wishes will be much easier to have if it is not an imminent possibility. However, if you are already in poor health, it is not too late to have the conversation.

APPENDIX D

Assessing Finances and Preparing A Plan

We sing "Praise God from whom all blessings flow," and yet we often lose touch with the reality that all blessings in life are a gift from God including our wealth. Whether our wealth is large or small, we have a responsibility to be good stewards throughout life. As we enter the later phase of life we may wonder, *Do I have enough? Will I outlive my funds? Am I prepared for the unexpected?*

These are not easy questions to answer. They take faith and wise counsel, not just from a financial planner, but from other Christians who can give input as to how faith and love of God can find expression in the way we manage our finances. Underlying all of our planning are the key questions:

- *Does our use of wealth increase the capacity for others to be blessed?*
- *Have I provided for the continued blessing of others after my death?*

Although it is desirable to be engaged in financial planning during all of one's adult life, it is especially important to give this area attention during the middle age years. Some of the key steps to take include:

1. Take an inventory of your financial resources
2. Design a retirement income strategy
3. Prepare a projected budget for later years
4. Anticipate the unexpected

5. Review your will and/or trust (and if you don't have a will, NOW is the time)

There are many tools available today through secular financial institutions to help with the details of financial planning, but it is the Christian community—found in churches and other Christian organizations including Christian financial services—that can provide the needed input for making choices that will be God-honoring. Early planning allows one to continue living as a good steward of God's resources all the days of one's life and beyond.

APPENDIX E

Adapting Housing for Accessibility

Aging in place is increasingly becoming the desired approach among the sixty-five and older population. People want to stay in the communities where they have built relationships and often in the homes where they made their life's memories.

For many, moving to an "accessible" home may not be a feasible option from a financial perspective or desire to retain social connections, so thinking through adaptations that could be made in an existing home may be the best first step.

We go to the doctor for regular check-ups. Why not pursue a "residence accessibility" check-up? A simple accessibility checklist might include discerning ways to create:

- ✓ Use of stairs for access to other levels
- ✓ Open walkways and hallways
- ✓ Wide doorways
- ✓ Pathways for ramps to outside
- ✓ Safety in the bathroom
- ✓ Ease in use of kitchen and laundry

If one is seeking to buy or rent a residence in a new location, a "what to look for" checklist will help narrow the potentials. The "accessibility" checklist noted above can be used for assessing the residence, but one needs to also determine if the location provides:

- ✓ Safety and security
- ✓ Sense of community
- ✓ Affordable economy
- ✓ Available work and volunteer opportunities
- ✓ Public transportation
- ✓ Accessible healthcare services

The design and location of a residence can negatively impact one's health and well-being if it hinders fulfilling daily tasks and/or limits socialization. The old adage applies to preparing for accessible living: *Don't put off until tomorrow what can be done today.*

REFERENCES

2016 *Alzheimer's Disease Facts and Figures.* Alzheimer's Association.

AARP *Public Policy Institute and National Conference of State Legislatures Research Report*, 2011.

"Ageism." *Dictionary.com.* Random House Unabridged Dictionary, 2015. Web. May. 2016.

Andrew J. Martin, Harry Nejad, Susan Colmar and Gregory Arief D. Liem (2012). *Adaptability: Conceptual and Empirical Perspectives on Responses to Change, Novelty and Uncertainty.* Australian Journal of Guidance and Counselling, 22, pp 58-81. doi:10.1017/jgc.2012.8.

"Andy Stanley." *BrainyQuote*. Xplore. Web. 2016.

Barna, George and Kinnaman, David. Churchless:*"Understanding Today's Unchurched and How to Connect with Them."* October 1 2014. Print.

Boice, James Montgomery. Daniel: An Expositional Commentary. 2003. Print.

Brenner, Joanna, and Aaron Smith. *"72% of Online Adults Are Social Networking Site Users."* Pew Research Center Internet Science Tech RSS. Pew Research Center, 05 Aug. 2013. Web. 6 June 2016

Bridges, William. *Managing Transitions: Making Sense of Life's Changes.* 2004. DeCapo Press, division of Peresus Books. Cambridge, MA

"*Canadian Longitudinal Study on Aging.*" Web. June 2016.

Chittister, Joan. *The Gift of Years: Growing Older Gracefully.* New York, NY: BlueBridge, 2008. Print.

Crosby, Franny. "To God Be the Glory." *Hymnary.org*. The Hymn Society, 2007. Web. 2016.

Cumming, Elaine, and William E. Henry. *Growing Old.* New York: Arno, 1961. Print.

"Dave Workman." *BrainyQuote*. Xplore. Web. 2016.

De Pree, Max. *Leadership Is an Art*. East Lansing, MI: Michigan State U, 1987. Print.

Dweck, Carol S. *Mindset: The New Psychology of Success*. New York: Random House, 2006. Print.

Erikson, Erik H. *Childhood and Society*. New York: Norton, 1964. Print.

Erikson, Erik H. and Erikson, Joan. *The Life Cycle Completed (Extended Version)*. New York: Norton, 1998. Print.

"Farshad Asl." *BrainyQuote*. Xplore. Web. 2016.

Foster, Richard J. *Celebration of Discipline*. London: Hodder & Stoughton, 1980. Print.

Gladwell, Malcolm. *Outliers: The Story of Success*. New York: Little, Brown, 2008. Print.

Hanson, Amy. *Baby Boomers and Beyond: Tapping the Ministry Talents and Passions of Adults over Fifty*. San Francisco, CA: Jossey-Bass, 2010. Print.

"Jason Silva." *BrainyQuote*. Xplore. Web. 2016.

"John F. Kennedy." *BrainyQuote*. Xplore. Web. 2016.

Larkin, Marilyn "Brain and Behavior Are Modifiable, Even as We Get Older." Elsevier Connect. May 2015. Web. June 2016. Columbia Aging Center at Columbia University.

"NetWellness." NetWellness. University of Ohio, n.d. Web. May 2016.

"Niko Kazantzakis." *BrainyQuote*. Xplore. Web. 9 Oct. 2015.

Nouwen, Henri J. M. *Life of the Beloved: Spiritual Living in a Secular World*. Crossroads Publishing. 1992. New York, NY. Print.

Nouwen, Henri J. M. *Lifesigns: Intimacy, Fecundity, and Ecstasy in Christian Perspective*. Garden City. N.Y.: Doubleday, 1986. Print.

Ortman, Jennifer M., Victoria A. Velkoff, and Howard Hogan. *"An Aging Nation: The Older Population in the United States."* U.S. Census Bureau. U.S. Census Bureau, May 2014. Web. June 2016.

Palmer, Parker J. *Let Your Life Speak: Listening for the Voice of Vocation*. San Francisco: Jossey-Bass, 2000. Print.'

"Ralph Waldo Emerson." *BrainyQuote*. Xplore. Web. Oct. 2015.

"Retirement." *Dictionary.com*. Random House Unabridged Dictionary, 2015. Web. November. 2015.

"Social Security History." *Social Security*. Social Security Administration, 11 Apr. 2012. Web. 2015.

Ten Boom, Corrie, John L. Sherrill, and Elizabeth Sherrill. *The Hiding Place*. Washington Depot, CT: Chosen, 1971. Print.

The English Standard Version Bible. New York: Oxford University Press, 2009. Print.

"The Holy Bible." New International Version. Grand Rapids, MI: Zondervan Corporation, 2010. Web. Oct. 2015.

Tournier, Paul. *Learn to Grow Old*. New York: Harper & Row, 1972. Print.

"*Volunteering in 2014 : The Economics Daily.*" U.S. Bureau of Labor Statistics. U.S. Bureau of Labor Statistics, n.d. Web. June 2016.

Waldinger, Robert. "*What Makes a Good Life? Lessons from the Longest Study on Happiness*" Harvard University. Web. December 2015.

RESOURCES

Books

Being Mortal, 2014 from Henry Holt & Company, By Atul Gawande

Canoeing the Mountains, 2015 from IVP Books, By Tod Bolsinger

Disrupt Aging: A Bold New Path to Living Your Best Life at Every Age, April 2016, by JoAnn Jenkins, CEO of AARP

Falling Upward, A Spirituality for the Two Halves of Life, 2011, by Richard Rohr

Life Reimagined: Discovering Your New Life Possibilities, Sep 6, 2013, by Richard J. Leider and Alan M. Webber

Managing Oneself, 2008 from Harvard Business Review Classics, By Peter Drucker

Shaping a Life of Significance for Retirement, Jan 1, 2010, by Jack Hansen and Jerry P Haas

The Next America, 2015, by Paul Taylor and the PEW Research Center

Third Calling: What are you doing the rest of your life?, August 2016,by Richard and Leona Bergstrom

What Got You Here, Won't Get You There: How Successful People Become Even More Successful, 2007 from Hachette books, By Marshall Goldsmith

Websites

amyhanson.org

changingaging.com

encore.org

lifereimagined.aarp.org

milkeninstitute.org/centers/the-center-for-the-future-of-aging

nextavenue.org

re-ignite.net

Other Media

Brief But Spectacular, Creator: Steve Goldbloom. Videographer: Zach Land-Miller. Featuring: Flossie Lewis. PBS Newshour, April 5, 2016.

Purposeful Aging: A Model for a New Life Course, October 2015 Study by the Center for the Future of Aging, Paul Irving, Chair at www.milkeninstitute.org/publications/view/760

What Makes a Good Life? Lessons from the Longest Study on Happiness, YouTube, TED Talk Electronically Published 25 Jan. 2016.

IN REFLECTION

Writing and researching for this book has been a wondrous journey. In the year since we began to intentionally gather and organize our thoughts about the ministry of the church with those who are in or on the threshold of the next phase of life, our passion for and commitment to this area of ministry has continued to grow. It's been amazing to witness the increasing attention being given to raising consciousness regarding Baby Boomers moving into this phase of life. Every week, it seems there is a new article, updated statistics, and testimonies of persons rejecting the stereotypes of older adults. The theme among these news items is ***that living a vital life all the days of our lives is not only the desired outcome, but a feasible outcome of growing older.***

Our hope in writing this book is that we can encourage and equip pastors, staff ministers, and lay leaders to engage in a conversation about the possibilities for their churches. They can make a difference in the lives of those who are already post-retirement, as well as the many Baby Boomers who have the opportunity to discover their pathways into this next phase of life. As these persons are regenerated, God will work in and through them to advance His mission.

We are deeply thankful to Reji Laberje for initiating the idea of putting our thoughts on paper and providing the "know how" needed and, we are grateful to her whole team for their support in publication. We have rejoiced in the many persons who have prayed with us and been open to hearing our thoughts.

In particular, we thank Millie Lungren and Debbie Blue, our long-time ministry colleagues, who invested time in reading the draft manuscript and helped us reorganize and refine. Their expertise helped at "just His right time." We also express gratitude to Carolyn Pitezel for the final review.

We are also deeply indebted to the models of vital living we have experienced throughout our lives. Special thanks is given to the contributors to the book—most of whom are from the West Coast and Chicago—where, together, we've had more recent ministries. These are persons who shared their vital life stories and wrote summaries of existing and emerging ministries. They have translated a vision into reality.

A listing of the persons giving Vital Life stories and locations of the existing and emerging ministries follows:

Vital Life Stories

Lenore Three Stars – Spokane, Washington

Will Davidson – San Ramon, California

Jim Gaderlund – Los Altos, California

Sharon Stenger – Roseville, California

Jorge Maldonado – Spring Valley, California

Sharon Davis – Chicago, Illinois

Allan and Joyce Anderson – Santa Barbara, California

Stanley Long – Fremont, California

Paul Larsen – Rancho Mirage, California
Rod Toews – Turlock, California
Marv Gibbs – Hong Kong

Existing and Emerging Ministries
PLUS –Redwood City, California
TREK –Gig Harbor, Washington
JOURNEYS – New Brighton, Minnesota
WITH AGE… - Chicago, Illinois
AN INSIDE LOOK AT AGING – Los Altos, California

We are forever grateful for God's gift of family and, in particular, supportive spouses (Sara who continues modeling vitality just as her mother Isabelle did and Phil, now among the cloud of witnesses). Without the reality of our freedom to "fly here and there," these thirty years of partnering in ministry might not have been possible. The years of partnering have provided the experiences and persons that are reflected in this book. Together we have served with the Evangelical Covenant Church, our denominational family that is committed to joining God in His mission to see more disciples, among more populations, in a more caring and just world. We are thankful for our denomination's efforts to address sexism and racism in the past fifty years. Now is the time for, not only the Evangelical Covenant Church, but all church bodies to address ageism as well. Let's join the pioneers who are blazing a new trail and create a movement.

"TO GOD BE THE GLORY, GREAT THINGS HE HATH DONE..." AND, GREAT THINGS HE IS DOING AND WILL DO....

About the Authors

Dr. Alan Forsman

Alan, currently residing in Sarasota, Florida, has over thirty years of experience in organizational consulting. He specializes in executive coaching, as well as team development, facilitation, and training.

Alan is coaching several executives from a variety of disciplines. He has taken substantial coursework in gerontology and started four older adult ministries while serving churches as a pastoral counselor and educator. In addition, he has consulted with several churches in starting significant older adult ministries. Alan has taught adult ministries and older adult ministries at the seminary level.

Alan is married to Sara and they have lived in seven states. Regeneration for Alan and Sara comes, not just from their active lives of service, but also from more than twenty nieces and nephews who keep them abreast of current trends while providing mutual mentoring and interacting around life skills and technology assistance.

Evelyn M.R. Johnson

Evelyn, currently residing in Chicago, Illinois, is an ordained minister in the Evangelical Covenant Church. She recently stepped aside from traditional compensated employment after serving for forty-two years in local church, regional conference, and denominational roles. Prior to returning to Chicago in August 2010 for a series of part-time denominational roles, Evelyn served as Superintendent of the Pacific Southwest Conference.

Evelyn is passionate about visioning for the future and translating that vision to action for the purpose of advancing Kingdom-building ministry. Evelyn loves to assist persons in navigating changes with a focus on living joyfully through transitions.

Evelyn was married to Phil, ten years older than her, for almost fifty-two years at the time of his death in 2014. She has two married sons (a Baby Boomer and a Generation Xer), two daughters-in-law (a Baby Boomer and a Generation Xer), and four grandchildren (all Millennials). Email, texting and social media are definitely a part of her vital life!

Reji Laberje

Working with Evelyn and Alan to create this "vital story," was Reji Laberje, Owner and Creative Director of Reji Laberje Writing and Publishing, where they use meaningful writing to, for, and from you to make far-reaching positive impacts.

Reji's books, including those written with Dick Vitale, Bob Brenner, and other positivity endorsers, as well as children's books from #1 Sports Publisher, Triumph Books, are read by tens of thousands of readers. Reji's company stands behind bestsellers and storytellers, alike and working on faith-guided pieces such as ***"Regenerating Generations,"*** is truly a treasured honor. Reji appreciates being engaged in a Kingdom-centered purpose for her writing. As a Generation Xer, she is grateful to learn from Evelyn and Alan at the start of the "planning and preparation" stage.

Reji lives and serves in her community near Milwaukee, Wisconsin, alongside her active home of seven (plus her four pets).